PRAISE FOR THE
UNCOMMON JUNIOR HIGH GROUP STUDIES

The *Uncommon* Junior High curriculum will help God's Word to become real for your students.
Larry Acosta
Founder of the Hispanic Ministry Center, Urban Youth Workers Institute

The best junior high/middle school curriculum to come out in years.
Jim Burns, Ph.D.
President of HomeWord (www.homeword.com)

A rich resource that makes genuine connections with middle school students and the culture in which they live.
Mark W. Cannister
Professor of Christian Ministries, Gordon College, Wenham, Massachusetts

A landmark resource for years to come.
Chapman R. Clark, Ph.D.
Professor of Youth, Family and Culture, Fuller Theological Seminary

Great biblical material, creative interaction and *user friendly*! What more could you ask for? I highly recommend it!
Ken Davis
Author and Speaker (www.kendavis.com)

A fresh tool . . . geared to make a lasting imp
Paul Fleischmann
President and Co-founder of the National Network of Youth Ministries

The *Uncommon* Junior High curriculum capitalizes both GOD and TRUTH.
Monty L. Hipp
President, The C4 Group (www.c4group.nonprofitsites.com)

The *Uncommon* Junior High curriculum is truly cross-cultural.
Walt Mueller
Founder and President, Center for Parent/Youth Understanding (www.cpyu.org)

The creators and writers of this curriculum know and love young teens, and that's what sets good junior high curriculum apart from the mediocre stuff!

Mark Oestreicher
Author, Speaker and Consultant (www.markoestreicher.com)

This is serious curriculum for junior-highers! Not only does it take the great themes of the Christian faith seriously, but it takes junior-highers seriously as well.

Wayne Rice
Founder and Director, Understanding Your Teenager (www.waynerice.com)

The *Uncommon* Junior High curriculum fleshes out two absolute essentials for great curriculum: biblical depth and active learning.

Duffy Robbins
Professor of Youth Ministry, Eastern University, St. Davids, Pennsylvania

It's about time that curriculum took junior-highers and youth workers seriously.

Rich Van Pelt
President of Alongside Consulting, Denver, Colorado

The *Uncommon* Junior High curriculum will help leaders bring excellence to every lesson while enjoying the benefit of a simplified preparation time.

Lynn Ziegenfuss
Mentoring Project Director, National Network of Youth Ministries

THE OLD TESTAMENT

KARA POWELL
General Editor

Published by Gospel Light
Ventura, California, U.S.A.
www.gospellight.com
Printed in the U.S.A.

Unit 1, "In the Beginning," previously published as Pulse #10: *Genesis.*
Unit 2, "Heroes of the Faith," sessions 8–10 previously published as sessions 1–3 in
Pulse #6: *Teens of the Bible.* Unit 2 sessions 7, 11 and 12 never before published.

Contributing writers: Kara Powell, PhD, Christi Goeser, Duffy Robbins,
Patti Pennington Virtue, Dave Zovak and Kim Zovak.

Library of Congress Cataloging-in-Publication Data
The Old Testament / Kara Powell, general editor.
p. cm. — (Uncommon jr. high group study)
ISBN 978-0-8307-5643-8 (trade paper)
1. Bible. O.T.—Study and teaching. 2. Christian education of teenagers. I. Powell, Kara.
BS1193.O38 2010
221.6071'2—dc22

Rights for publishing this book outside the U.S.A. or in non-English languages are
administered by Gospel Light Worldwide, an international not-for-profit ministry.
For additional information, please visit www.glww.org, email info@glww.org, or write
to Gospel Light Worldwide, 1957 Eastman Avenue, Ventura, CA 93003, U.S.A.

To order copies of this book and other Gospel Light products in bulk quantities,
please contact us at 1-800-446-7735.

Contents

How to Use the Uncommon Junior High Group Studies

Each *Uncommon* junior high group study contains 12 sessions, which are divided into 2 stand-alone units of 6 sessions each. You may choose to teach all 12 sessions consecutively, or to use just one unit, or to present each session separately. You know your group, so do what works best for you and your students.

This is your leader's guidebook for teaching your group. Electronic files (in PDF format) for each session's student handouts are available online at **www.gospellight.com/uncommon/jh_the_old_testament.zip**. The handouts include the "Reflect" section of each study, formatted for easy printing, in addition to any student worksheets for the session. You may print as many copies as you need for your group.

Each individual session begins with a brief overview of the "big idea" of the lesson, the aims of the session, the primary Bible verse and additional verses that tie in to the topic being discussed. Each of the 12 sessions is geared to be 45 to 90 minutes in length and is comprised of two options that you can choose from, based on the type of group that you have. Option 1 tends to be a more active learning experience, while Option 2 tends to be a more discussion-oriented exercise.

The sections in each session are as follows:

Starter
Young people will stay in your youth group longer if they feel comfortable and make friends. This first section helps students get to know each other better and focus on the theme of the lesson in a fun and engaging way.

Message
The Message section enables students to look up to God by relating the words of Scripture to the session topic.

Dig

Unfortunately, many young people are biblically illiterate. In this section, students look inward and discover how God's Word connects with their own world.

Apply

Young people need the opportunity to think through the issues at hand. The apply section leads students out into their world with specific challenges to apply at school, at home and with their friends.

Reflect

This concluding section of the study allows students to reflect on the material presented in the session. You can print these pages from the PDF found at www.gospellight.com/uncommon/jh_the_new_testament.zip and give them to your students as a handout for them to work on throughout the week.

Want More Options?

An additional option for each section, along with accompanying worksheets, is available in PDF format at www.gospellight.com/uncommon/jh_the_old_testament.zip.

UNIT I

In the Beginning

As a junior-higher, I loved hearing stories about myself when I was younger. I begged my mom to tell me about the puppet shows my brother and I did when we were five and seven years old. (I, of course, always had the lead role.) I eagerly listened as Mom told stories about the sheet forts we made in our living room to protect ourselves from the rolled up "sock bombs" we threw at each other (the more pillows and sheets the better). I was tickled when I heard about the time my third-grade class went whale watching and most of us ended up getting sick over the side of the boat (real high-class, junior high humor).

I don't think I'm the only junior-higher who delighted in hearing stories about myself. Sure, there are childhood memories I, and others, would rather forget, but most junior-highers enjoy reliving those funny, significant or memorable moments again and again and again. They love hearing about their own beginnings.

So, if all that's true, then why aren't young teens clamoring to hear more about the ultimate beginning? In Genesis, God has left us all sorts of fascinating stories about relationships, disasters and murders to retell and relive, and yet, most sixth, seventh and eighth graders greet them with a yawn.

Maybe it's because junior-highers think the chapters of Genesis are fables—that they are not really true. Given what they are taught about evolution in their science classes, they may have concluded that the stories of Genesis are just cute fairy tale stories.

But if the veracity of the Genesis account is really the reason behind junior-highers' lack of interest, why do they flock to the latest animated or computer-generated fables in the movie theatres? Or the newest fictitious computer game? Movie ticket revenue and merchandise sales suggest that a story doesn't have to be true to captivate junior-highers.

Influenced by the postmodern mindset surrounding us, many students seem to care less about whether something is *true* and more about whether it's *relevant*. And, frankly, too many junior high ministries have allowed the stories of Genesis to become remnants from a distant, flannel board past.

As junior high youth workers desiring something more, we've carefully designed this first unit to show junior-highers both the *truth* and the *relevancy* of the beginnings in Genesis:

- **Vivid illustrations:** We've provided easy-to-do and hard-to-forget visual illustrations to reinforce the main points of each session.

- **Clear applications:** No junior-higher should be able to walk away wondering what difference sin or faith or deliverance makes in his or her life. As their leader, you have two creative and tangible application options to choose from for each lesson (a third option is available in the "additional options" pdf found at **www.gospellight.com/uncommon_jh_the_old_testament.zip**).

- **Three-dimensional characters:** We will intentionally show you the humanity of Adam and Eve and the mistakes Joseph made. The heroes of Genesis weren't superhuman saints but ordinary people who tried, and sometimes failed, to follow an extraordinary God—just as your junior-highers do (and, frankly, just as you do).

Thank God for the wonderful beginnings He gave us, first in Genesis and second in Jesus Christ.

Kara Powell
Executive Director of the Fuller Youth Institute
Assistant Professor of Youth, Family and Culture
Fuller Theological Seminary

GOD: THE BEGINNING OF CREATION

THE BIG IDEA
God specially designed all of creation, including us!

SESSION AIMS
In this session you will guide students to (1) establish that God alone created the universe; (2) feel affirmed that they were specially and carefully designed by God; and (3) accept the challenge to enjoy a living relationship with their Creator this week.

THE BIGGEST VERSE
"In the beginning God created the heavens and the earth. Now the earth was formless and empty, darkness was over the surface of the deep, and the Spirit of God was hovering over the waters" (Genesis 1:1-2).

OTHER IMPORTANT VERSES
Genesis 1:1-31; 2:7; Job 41:1; Psalms 24:1-2; 74:13-14; 121:7-8; 139:13-16; 148:5; Isaiah 27:1; Jeremiah 31:3; Matthew 11:28; John 1:1-3; 17:23; Romans 1:19-20; Hebrews 11:3,6; 1 Peter 3:15; 2 Peter 3:10-13

Note: Additional options and worksheets in 8$^1/_2$" x 11" format for this session are available for download at **www.gospellight.com/uncommon/jh_the_old_testament.zip**.

STARTER

Option 1: Tangled Yarn. For this option, you will need three different-colored strands of yarn, each approximately 36 inches long. You will also need three keys and a whistle. Ahead of time, attach a key to one end of each strand of yarn and loosely tangle all three strands of yarn together (leaving the other ends *without* keys attached hanging out) to form one large ball. (*Note*: The yarn needs to be tangled only enough to make it difficult to remove the ends that have the keys attached while keeping the keys well hidden.)

Welcome students and announce that you're beginning this session with a contest. Divide the students into three teams and assign each team a color corresponding to the yarn you've tangled. Line students up single file, and instruct them to sit down in that order. When you blow the whistle, the first person on each team will come forward and try to find the beginning of his or her team's assigned color of yarn by untangling it from the rest of the colors (only you know that there's a key attached). Allow 15 seconds for team members to attempt to free their colors. Blow the whistle again for them to stop, at which time the next three contestants come forward. Repeat the process until every student has come forward or until one team untangles the yarn and locates its key.

Congratulate the winning team and ask the following questions:

- What was the hardest part about untangling your team's yarn? (*Not knowing where the yarn began or ended; it was all tangled with the other teams' yarn.*)

- What needed to happen in order to find the key on the end of the yarn? (*You needed to figure out where the yarn piece started.*)

Explain that there are a lot of tangled ideas out there about the way life began. The key to unraveling the truth from all those ideas is to go all the way back to the beginning and get the facts. The Bible tells us that God specifically created this world (see Genesis 1:1). It wasn't by chance; it wasn't arbitrary. Today we're going to see that God made heaven and earth—including you—with special and careful thought.

Option 2: How Did It Start? For this option, you will need one copy of "How Did It Start?" (found on the next page) and a container (a small basket or a bowl—even a baseball cap works well). Ahead of time, cut apart the six endings from "How Did It Start?" and place them in the container.

How Did It Start?

STORY-ENDING ONE
Then Prince Charming put the glass slipper on her foot. It fit! His search was over! He took her back to the royal castle and married her and they lived happily ever after.

STORY-ENDING TWO
They marched around seven times, blowing their trumpets and shouting. The walls of the city came crashing down.

STORY-ENDING THREE
As they walked up the hill to the widow's house, Tom and Huck planned their next big adventure.

STORY-ENDING FOUR
He finally ate the green eggs and ham and thanked the pesky Sam-I-am!

STORY-ENDING FIVE
They threw her down, and her blood splattered the wall and the horses as they trampled her underfoot. When they went to bury her, they found nothing but her skull, feet and hands.

STORY-ENDING SIX
Jonah finally understood that God is merciful, wise and all-forgiving.

Greet students and ask if they think they could recognize a story just by hearing the end of it. Choose a volunteer to draw one of the slips of paper from the container and ask her to read it aloud to the group. Instruct students to raise their hands as soon as they recognize the story that the ending completes. Call on the first student. If his answer is not correct, ask another student whose hand is raised. (*Note:* The story endings are from [1] *Cinderella,* [2] the battle of Jericho from Joshua 6, [3] *The Adventures of Tom Sawyer,* [4] *Green Eggs and Ham,* [5] Jezebel's death from 2 Kings 9, and [6] Jonah 4.)

Continue the process until all six slips of paper have been selected and read, and then discuss the following:

- What made some of the stories easier to recognize than others? (*The easy ones were those in which we knew the beginning and the characters.*)

- How does knowing the beginning of something change your understanding of it? (*Knowing how something starts gives you a better idea of how everything fits together and why things are the way they are.*)

- Have you ever walked into a room in the middle of a discussion and had no clue what was being talked about? Or have you ever returned to class after being absent from school for a few days and felt a little bit lost? How did it affect your ability to join in? (*Felt clueless and confused; couldn't join in; didn't understand what was going on.*)

- How would you feel about being dumped into an advanced calculus class the day of the final exam? (*No fair. I'd walk. I'd call my lawyer!*)

- What would be tough about that? (*I wouldn't have studied the beginning but would be expected to produce results in the end.*)

- Okay, here's one for you: We see creation and life all around us. Where did it all come from? (*You should get some interesting responses, but don't affirm or discount any of them yet—that's for the next step.*)

Youth Leader Tip

Sorting through the issues of biblical faith and evolution is impossible in one session. The main point you want to stress is that the universe came about as the result of the purposeful will of the almighty God.

Transition to the next step by explaining that there is one story that they *need* to know from the beginning because it's how we came to be. It's the true story of creation from the first book in the Bible, Genesis. This is a book all about beginnings: the beginning of the universe, the beginning of people, the beginning of faith in God. In order to really make sense out of life today, we need to go back and look at how it all started, just as reading the beginning of a book allows us to really understand and appreciate the rest of it.

MESSAGE

Option 1: Something from Nothing. For this option, you will need several Bibles, two boxes filled with an assortment of odds and ends that could be used to create something (such as scraps of wood, rope, cups, bicycle inner-tubes, pieces from broken appliances, duct tape—basically, you need to raid a cluttered garage and see what you can come up with!), and one flower for each student, the more unusual the better. (*Caution:* Don't go picking Mrs. Brown's prized roses without asking her first!)

Divide students into two groups, and place one box in the middle of each group. Tell students to wait for your signal to dive into the contents of their boxes and try to construct something useful. Allow several minutes and then signal for groups to stop. Let each group present its creation and explain its use. After this amazing display of junior high genius, discuss the following:

- Were you satisfied with your creation? Why or why not?
- What would you change about it to make it even better?

Explain that when we think about the creation of the world, we often gloss over the immense power that God showed as He designed and crafted it and everything in it. *No detail was overlooked.* God made all things in a thought-out and meaningful way. Yet there was something even more remarkable about the way He created the world.

Read Genesis 1:1-2 and Hebrews 11:3 aloud and continue by stating that when the Bible says that God "created the heavens and the earth" (meaning everything), it literally means He made *something out of nothing.*[1] He didn't just scoop up some things from His heavenly garage and tinker around with them until He ended up making something that actually worked. He took emptiness and filled it. He caused things to exist that had never before existed. Illustrate this abstract idea by holding up the now empty boxes. Ask, "What if I had told you to create something out of the contents of this empty box, would you have been able to do it? No!" Continue by stating that this is exactly what God did when He created the world—He created something out of nothing.

Ask volunteers to read the following Scripture passages aloud: Genesis 1:26-27, Genesis 2:7, Psalms 24:1-2 and 148:5. Afterward, explain that one of the most obvious reasons to believe that God is the Creator of all things is the great design that exists in our world. As you talk, distribute a flower to each student. Continue by stating that the complexity of creation reveals that there was a master designer at work. Even something as simple as this flower shows the power and creativity of a designer. Our world didn't just happen by accident. You and I are not here merely because some non-living chemicals bumped into each other and combined over a long period of time into a complex, completely amazing individual. Someone planned it and had the power to make it a reality. That someone is Jesus Christ. Conclude by reading John 1:1-3.

Option 2: Typing Blind. For this option, you will need several Bibles, a typewriter (the older the better), typing paper, three self-stick nametags, a felt-tip pen and three blindfolds. (*Note:* If you can't find a typewriter, you could also use a computer and a printer.) Ahead of time, label the nametags Chemical A, Chemical B and Chemical C.

Show students the typewriter (some of them may never have seen one!) and insert a sheet of blank paper. Invite three volunteers to come to the front and give each of them one of the nametags to wear. Blindfold them and ask them to each place one hand on the typewriter keys and their other hand behind their back. When you give the signal, they are to begin typing at the same time. Let them type for about one minute, and then signal them to stop. Take the blindfolds off and invite them to return to their seats.

Distribute Bibles and explain that one of the key ideas behind the theory of evolution is that life came from nonlife; that nonliving chemicals randomly came together and somehow started a single-celled living organism. Over billions of years, these single-celled organisms evolved from one life form to another, until we ended up with a human being. Explain that this would be similar to what we just saw: some chemicals randomly assembling a message on this typewriter and ending up with the complete works of William Shakespeare. Now try to read what they wrote by sounding out the letters and exaggerating the process.

Hand the paper to a few students to see if they can read anything, and then discuss the following questions:

- Is evolution based on scientific fact? (*Science is wonderful—it brings us new and exciting discoveries every day. Scientific theories are based on interpretations of observations—and those theories might become accepted as scientific facts. For instance, a scientist who seeks to prove the basic theory of evolution—that all life is the result of a blind combination of time, chance and matter and that no Creator was needed—may only consider evidence that supports his or her theory and discount the awesome evidence that God is the Creator and Designer of every living thing.*)

- Can scientists prove *any* theory of evolution that excludes God as the Creator and Designer of all life? (*Science cannot disprove the existence of God in any area! The Bible clearly says God spoke and the world was created—His Word created everything alive [see Psalm 148:5]. We don't know exactly how He did it, but we can be sure that He is the one who did!*)

- Do fossils prove the theory of evolution? (*Nope! No one has ever dug up a fossil of an animal that hadn't quite finished evolving from a fish into a bird or an ape in the process of becoming a man. Genesis 1:24 says that God created "each according to its kind." God created a variety of plant and animal life, so there are all sorts of fossils to be found, but none of them can prove that one animal evolved from another.*)

- Why doesn't the Bible mention dinosaurs? (*Actually, the Bible does describe a huge creature called a leviathan in Job 41:1; Psalm 74:13-14 and Isaiah 27:1. This was perhaps a dinosaur, though no one can be absolutely sure. However, you won't find a platypus or kangaroo mentioned by name either! The Bible is not a science book—and it wasn't intended to be. Its purpose is to teach us about God and His awesome plan for us.*)

Read Romans 1:19-20, and then discuss the following:

- What does Paul mean when he says, "God has made it plain to them"? (*Creation itself shows us that some higher intelligence exists. No one can look at the world and honestly deny that there is a God who created it.*)

- What are some of God's invisible qualities? (*Things about Him we can't see except through what He created, such as His creativity.*)

- What part of God's creation demonstrates His power to you? His wisdom? His creativity?

Continue by stating that of all God created, the crowning work of His creation is humanity, which includes *us*! Only humans were made in His image. Read Genesis 1:1-3,26-27; 2:7, and then explain that being made in God's image doesn't necessarily mean that we look like God in our physical appearance. Rather, we have been given a spiritual nature that reflects, in a small measure, the character and nature of God Himself. This gives us the unique ability to have an eternal relationship with God. We are different from animals, stars and plants because we can enjoy fellowship with God, friend to friend. Read Genesis 1:31 and conclude by telling the group that each one of them is God's work of art.[2]

DIG

Option 1: Switch Up. For this option, you will need just this book and some talkative students! Read part 1 of the following scenario, but don't let students know that there are two parts.

James had been saving money since he could remember to buy a car when he turned 16. His birthday was two weeks away; and he had $7,000 to spend—$3,500 that he had saved, plus $3,500 his dad had agreed to give him. He was really excited on Wednesday when he saw an advertisement for a local car dealer showing a used Camaro for $6,500. His dad was very busy that week, but promised to take him on the weekend to look at the car. Anxiously, James prayed that it would still be there on the weekend.

James's best friend, Ricky, called on Friday to congratulate him on his new car, but James had no idea what Ricky was talking about. Ricky explained that he had seen James's dad at the car dealer looking at a new Mitsubishi Eclipse and a used Hyundai. Ricky was sure that the Hyundai was for James because he saw the price sticker on the window—$3,500.

Youth Leader Tip
Always try to keep to the topic so that you can clearly finish the teaching. Encourage your group members' curiosity by having a time for questions on related topics at the end or after the session.

Later that evening, while his mom and dad were out, James was looking for a pen on his dad's desk when he came across two receipts: one for a brand-new Eclipse and one for a used Hyundai. He knew he should be grateful, but he couldn't help feeling disappointed. His dad was using the money he promised James on a new car for *himself!* The more James thought about it, the more hurt and angry he became.

Now discuss the following:

- How would you feel if you were James? (*Upset, angry.*)
- What would you think about the dad's actions? (*He's selfish; he didn't keep his promise.*)
- Based on the facts and what James's friend told him, he'd be pretty justified in feeling disappointed and upset, wouldn't he? (*Yes!*)

Now ask the group what they would think if you told them that James didn't really know the facts. What if you told them that he was making a judgment based on observation, not fact? Now read part 2:

When his parents arrived home, James was already in bed, pretending to be asleep. He heard them whispering and curiosity got the best of him, so he sat up and listened. His dad said, "I know he wanted the Camaro, but I really think this is a better deal in the long run."

James thought, *Well, it sure saved him a hefty amount, didn't it?*

"I know we should wait for his birthday, but I just can't. I'm glad we were able to pick it up tonight. And I'm so happy with mine! It'll be nice to have one of my own again," his mom replied.

My mom's getting the new one? I really rate around here, don't I?

James went to sleep, and when he woke up early the next morning, he went downstairs to eat. He sat in the kitchen, eating his cereal and thinking about how life isn't fair. Soon his dad and mom came into the kitchen. James grumbled, "Good morning," with a mouthful of cereal. His dad asked him to come out into the garage. *Here we go,* James thought. *I'd better act surprised.*

As he stepped into the garage, James saw a huge ribbon tied to the hood of the Eclipse with the words "Happy Birthday" written on the windshield! He couldn't believe his eyes! His mom and dad gave him a hug, and his mom proudly showed him her new car too. She was *so* happy with her Hyundai—definitely more grateful than James had been when he thought it was his.

Explain that James reacted to what he believed to be the facts—but the only *true* facts are the ones that show what's happened from every angle. The theory of evolution is like that. It's a theory based purely on scientific observation—what scientists *see* as fact, substituting an anti-God belief for true science. God is the only one who can truly see all the facts from every angle, and we can ask Him to help us understand the truth.

Option 2: God's Will and Other Questions. For this option, you will need just these questions! Discuss the following with the group:

- If God created everything perfectly, how can there be evil in the world? (*God designed and created everything perfectly, but when Adam and Eve sinned, they allowed God's perfect world to become tainted by misery and sorrow. In 2 Peter 3:10-13, we read about a day when God will create a new heaven and a new earth, where the effects of sin will be wiped out and we will again enjoy a world in the way God originally intended.*)

- If I'm so wonderful, why do I feel so bad? (*Actually, there are a lot of things that affect how we feel about ourselves. A huge part of our emotional makeup is hormones—and junior-highers are full of those! We are also affected by what others tell us—rightly or wrongly—about ourselves. We need to recognize that God doesn't base His love for us—or His approval of us—upon our own or others' assessments of ourselves.*)

- If my purpose is to have a relationship with God, why do I feel He never listens to me? (*God is always listening. The problem might be that we need to sit down long enough to hear His answer! In addition, the hard part is realizing that His answer is sometimes "no" or "wait awhile."*)

- How do I know if I'm doing what God wants me to do with my life? (*There won't be a huge sign descending from heaven that says, "You go, girl!" But you will know that you're doing what He wants you to do when you are truly seeking to please Him by glorifying Him with your life. You don't have to go into paid ministry to serve God and have fellowship with*

Him every day. No matter what your job is or how old you are, you can serve Him with the gifts He's given you.)

APPLY

Option 1: How Much Am I Worth? You will need several Bibles, copies of "How Much Am I Worth?" (found on the next page), and pens or pencils.

This may be the first time that some of your students have ever really thought about their significance as God's crowning creation. Challenge them to respond to this idea by looking a little deeper into the Word and reflecting upon what it says about their value to God. If possible, pair up stronger believers with those who are on the periphery of faith in Christ so that this exercise is a seed-sowing time.

Explain that you are very valuable to God and He loves you more deeply and faithfully than you could ever imagine. Distribute "How Much Am I Worth?" and allow approximately 8 to 10 minutes for students to look up the Bible references. Regroup and give students the opportunity to really know God's love by accepting Jesus as their Lord. Close with prayer, asking God to affirm His love to each student there.

Option 2: The Combination. For this option, you will need a key for every student (unusable keys can be obtained, usually free of charge, from a locksmith). As an option, if you can't locate enough keys, photocopy pictures of keys onto cardstock, cut them apart and give the key cards to students. Now read the following scenario:

Recently you got a new combination for your locker. After arriving home on Friday afternoon, you realize you've forgotten your history book in your locker and you have a huge assignment due on Monday morning, first period. You can't go back to school and get your book because you've

Youth Leader Tip
You will have to set the tone for students to take this activity seriously. Set clear parameters for this time (no talking, no sleeping, no paper airplanes, no texting) and then lead by example!

How Much Am I Worth?

What made man come alive?
Genesis 2:7: "The LORD God formed the man from the _____ of the ground and breathed into his nostrils the breath of life, and the man became a living being."

What kind of love does God have for you?
Jeremiah 31:3: "I have loved you with an _____ love; I have drawn you with _____."

What is God watching over?
Psalm 121:7-8: "The LORD will keep you from all harm—he will watch over your life; the LORD will watch over your _____ and _____ both now and forevermore."

What has God promised to do if you come to Him with your worries?
Matthew 11:28: "Come to me, all you who are weary and burdened, and I will give you _____."

In order to come to God, what two things do we have to believe?
Hebrews 11:6: "And without faith it is impossible to please God, because anyone who comes to him must believe that he _____ and that he _____ those who earnestly seek him."

How much does God love you?
John 17:23: "I in them and you in me. May they be brought to complete unity to let the world know that you sent me and have loved them even as you have loved _____."

Prayer
Reread the verses above. Write a prayer to God based on these Scripture passages. What do you want to say to Him right now?

_____

_____

_____

_____

_____

forgotten your new combination. You spend all weekend preoccupied and worried about your assignment. On Monday morning you find out that your best friend had the combination memorized but didn't bother to tell you, even though he spent all of Saturday with you!

Ask the group how they would feel about their best friend not sharing the information they needed (*they would probably feel mad, upset and confused*). Explain to the group members that they now have the absolute truth about their existence—God created them! *They* hold the combination to unlocking the door to eternal life with Jesus Christ, not just for themselves, but for others as well. They can choose to keep it to themselves, or they can share it with others and allow them to open the door to the truth about themselves: God created them with loving thoughtfulness.

Read 1 Peter 3:15 and then divide students into groups of three to five. Ask them to pray for the opportunity to be bold in their defense of the truth. As students leave, distribute the keys and invite them to share the truth about creation with one person during the next week. They can give the key to the person and challenge him or her to do the same.

REFLECT

The following short devotions are for the students to reflect on and answer during the week. You can make a copy of these pages and distribute to your class or download and print from **www.gospellight.com/uncommon/jh_the_old_testament.zip.**

1—HIS PRIDE AND JOY

Psalm 139:13-16 is an amazing poem about what a special work of art you are to God. Take time to read it!

Have you ever been assigned an art or a science project in school? If you have, then you know that even before you start working on it, you must spend time planning and preparing to make or build the project. If the project is well planned and you have worked hard on it, it can be a source of pride and joy!

To have a better day, remember you are God's pride and joy. What are two examples that show this is true?

_____

_____

_____

Ask God to help you remember how much He delights in you today!

2—IN HIS IMAGE

Dig into Genesis 1:26-27.

Being made in God's image doesn't necessarily mean that we look like God in our *physical appearance*. It means we have been given a spiritual nature that reflects the character and nature of God Himself. This gives us the unique ability to have an eternal relationship with God. We are different from animals, stars and plants because we can enjoy fellowship with God, friend to friend.

Think about it. The Bible says that we were created *in the image of God*. Are we clones of God? Is that what being created in the image of God is about? (The answer is, *ABSOLUTELY NOT!*) So where is the image of God to be found?

Below is a list of some of God's qualities. Put a check next to each attribute that you find, in a much more limited way, in yourself.

☐ All-powerful   ☐ Creative
☐ All-knowing   ☐ Speaks the truth
☐ Loving   ☐ Artistic
☐ Thoughtful   ☐ Knows good from evil
☐ Good listener   ☐ Faithful
☐ Merciful   ☐ A servant

Now pick one attribute that you think God put in you so that you could re-flect His image in a special way. Then complete the following prayer: *Thank You, God, for making me special and in Your image so that I can be in a relationship with You. When I look in the mirror, I see Your image in me because . . .*

3—THE SOURCE

Hey! Go check out John 1:1-4,10-13.

If you stop feeding an animal, it will die. It you cut off a plant's light source, it will die. If you take a fish out of water, it will die. Without the source of life necessary to sustain each individual creation, it cannot survive. In a similar way, we each have a source of life: God our Creator, who made all things through Christ His Son. He keeps life going through His Spirit.

According to John 1:10-11, what is it that keeps the world from being con-nected to Jesus, the source of life?

_____

_____

_____

_____

What do you think will happen to those who remain unconnected to their source of life, God?

_____

_____

_____

_____

Spend a few minutes praying for two people you know who don't seem to be connected to God as their source of life.

4—RE-CREATED

Jump into what Paul says in Ephesians 2:10.

Jill was poking around in her grandmother's basement when she came across an interesting-looking but very dirty object. "What is this?" she asked her grandma.

"Why, that is an old crystal vase my father gave to my mother," Grandma exclaimed. "She would fill it with flowers and put it on his desk, but he mostly used it as a paperweight. I got it when my parents passed away, but your Uncle Sam used it to hold his rock collection. Somehow it just turned up in the basement. I had forgotten it even existed."

Jill took the vase home and cleaned it up, and now it sits on the coffee table, full of lovely flowers. That vase is back to being used for the purpose for which it was made. Just as that vase was made to hold flowers, God created people for a unique and personal purpose.

Although everyone is made in the image of God, those who ask Jesus to be their Savior are cleaned up from the inside out—re-created. God can then use them for the purpose He planned for them—a lot like Jill's flower vase that is back to holding flowers (which is what it was made for in the first place!).

What about you? Have you been re-created by inviting Jesus to be your Lord and Savior? If so, what are some of the good works that God may have prepared for you to do in the present?

_____

_____

_____

In the near future?

_____

_____

_____

In the distant future?

_____

_____

_____

_____

ADAM AND EVE: THE BEGINNING OF FAMILY

THE BIG IDEA

Families are God's idea and are meant to give us a sense of belonging.

SESSION AIMS

In this session you will guide students to (1) understand that families were God's idea; (2) realize that the desire to belong is meant to be satisfied within the context of a loving family; and (3) accept God as a heavenly Father whose love will be with them through the good times and the bad.

THE BIGGEST VERSE

"The Lord God said, 'It is not good for the man to be alone. I will make a helper suitable for him'" (Genesis 2:18).

OTHER IMPORTANT VERSES

Genesis 1:27; 2:18-24; 3; Exodus 18:4; Deuteronomy 33:29; Psalms 15:4; 33:20; 68:5-6; 10:14; Proverbs 15:25; Ecclesiastes 4:9-12; Jeremiah 49:11; Matthew 19:26; 22:37-39; John 1:12-13; Romans 5:12; 7:5,18; 8:15-16; Galatians 3:26; Ephesians 3:14-15; Philippians 2:13; 1 John 3:1

Note: Additional options and worksheets in 8$^1/_2$" x 11" format for this session are available for download at **www.gospellight.com/uncommon/jh_the_old_testament.zip**.

STARTER

Option 1: Freaky Families. For this option, you will need the opening segment of the old TV series *The Munsters* (you can find this on YouTube), where the different members of the family are introduced, and a way to play it to the group.

Welcome students and introduce the session by explaining that last week we took a look at how the world began and found out that God specifically designed the universe and everything in it, including *us.* This week, we'll look at how families began and discover that part of God's plan for us is that we belong to a loving group of people that will support and care for us no matter what. We were created to belong, not to be loners.

Show the movie clip introducing the Munster family members, and then discuss the following:

- In the Munster family, the blond-haired, blue-eyed niece is the strange one. Have you ever felt like you had the weirdest family on earth? (*Everyone has felt that way at some point.*)

- What is a family? (*It's a group of people who belong to each other, either by birth or choice, and who are committed to seeing each other succeed and prosper. If students don't suggest this, be sure to emphasize nontraditional family units that are so prevalent today.*)

- How has the idea of family changed over the years? (*One way to answer this is to help students think of famous TV families over the years. The 1950s had the stereotypical, traditional dad, mom and two or three kids in shows such as* Leave It to Beaver *and* Father Knows Best. *The 1960s began to show one parent or no-parent families in shows such as* Family Affair *and* The Andy Griffith Show. *The 1970s showed a mixture of family types in shows such as* All in the Family, The Partridge Family *and* The Brady Bunch. *The 1980s featured primarily dysfunctional families in shows such as* Dallas, The Simpsons *and* Married with Children. *The 1990s had a whole range of shows, ranging from traditional families in* Home Improvement *and* Seventh Heaven *to mixed families in* Party of Five *and* Dawson's Creek. *The 2000s gave us a live look at families—showing them at their best and at their worst—through reality shows such as* The Osbournes, Keeping up with the Kardashians, Wife Swap *and* Supernanny. *There is a pretty wide spectrum of family styles to choose from that definitely reflect a changing understanding of what a family is!*)

Explain that families are not just about people all having the same address. Families are about truly belonging to each other, about being a part of someone else's world and letting someone share yours. Ask the group what a perfect family would be like. Let students describe their ideas of perfect families, and then guide them to understand that everyone feels the need to belong to something. That feeling is a God-given desire and is meant to be satisfied first within the context of a family.

Conclude by stating that families are important. We laugh about them, cry about them, get mad at them, feel frustrated with them; but still, we need them. Families are God's idea and are meant to be a way for Him to bless us. Unfortunately, that doesn't always happen. Thirty percent of the children in our country do not live in a home with both parents, but that doesn't mean that they can't enjoy the blessings of family.[1] God, our perfect heavenly Father, is the one through whom we find all our needs and desires met. He is where all kinds of families—whether one parent, two parents or no parents—find the love and hope they need.

Option 2: Family Feud. For this option, you will need one copy of "Family Feud" (found on the next page), six blue and six red baseball caps (or bandanas), a bell or buzzer (the kind you might find on the counter at a hotel to get the clerk's attention), a table, a whiteboard, a dry-erase marker and prizes.

Welcome the students and introduce the session by explaining that during the last session, we learned how the world began and found out that God specifically designed the universe and everything in it, including *us*. Now we're going to look at how families began and discover that part of God's plan for us is to belong to a loving group of people that will support and care for us no matter what. We were created to belong, not to be loners.

Choose 12 volunteers and divide them into two teams. Give each team a family name and one of the sets of baseball caps (or bandanas). Have each family team form two single-file lines facing each other for a game of Family

Youth Leader Tip
The point to stress here is that what connects a family is the love the members have for one another. Even if this has not been true of the students' earthly families, the love of their Father God for them is unyeilding.

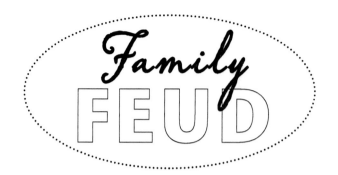

Questions	*Answers*
Name the middle daughter in *The Brady Bunch*.	Jan
Where does Fred Flintstone work?	At a rock quarry
Where does the First Family live?	In the White House
How many members in the Simpsons family live at home?	Five
What are the given names of Ward and June Cleaver's sons?	Wally and Theodore
Name the members of the Jetson family.	George, Jane, Judy and Elroy
What does every season of *Survivor* feature that often makes the participants break down and cry?	A visit from a family member
What is the name of the dad in the Addams family?	Gomez
On *SpongeBob SquarePants*, what is the name of Mr. Krabs's daughter?	Pearl
What was the name of the show in which a man adopted the two orphaned sons of his former housekeeper?	*Different Strokes*
Opie was raised by a single dad in what show?	*The Andy Griffith Show*

Feud. Place the bell on a table between the first two volunteers. Instruct them to place both hands behind their backs as you read the first question. If a person thinks she knows the answer, she can swing her arm around and ring the bell. However, if the bell is hit before you have time to finish the question, the person who rang it must finish the question first and then give the answer. Award 500 points for a correct answer and use the whiteboard to keep each family's running total. If a contestant answers incorrectly, the other family gets a chance to answer and win the points. If no one is able to give a correct answer, no points are awarded (you can give the audience a chance to answer the question). Total the points at the end of the game and award prizes to the winning family.

Close by explaining that families are important. We laugh about them, cry about them, get mad at them, feel frustrated with them; but still, we need them. Families were God's idea and are meant to be a way for Him to bless us. Unfortunately, that doesn't always happen. Thirty percent of the children in our country do not live in a home with both parents, but that doesn't mean that they can't enjoy the blessings of family.[2] God, our perfect heavenly Father, is the One through whom we find all our needs and desires met. He is where all kinds of families—whether one parent, two parents or no parents—find the love and hope they need.

MESSAGE

Option 1: Family Photo. For this option, you will need several Bibles and a family photo that shows a clear family physical resemblance (this might be a photo of your own or someone else's family—it's important that there be a strong resemblance for this option to work).

Begin by asking the group how many of them plan on being married someday. (Pokes in the ribs and snickers abound.) Now ask how they will know who is the right person to marry. What kinds of qualities will they look for in a mate? (*Note:* Be careful not to get sidetracked on this question. Just allow students to briefly describe some qualities they would look for in a spouse.) Continue by stating that many statistics show fewer people are getting married now than ever before in U.S. history. Why do they think this is true? (*Fear of commitment, lack of successful examples, too risky, too demanding.*)

Explain that when God created "man" in His image, He made two people—not just a man but also a woman (see Genesis 1:27). It took both of them together to even begin to reflect the beauty of God's nature. We are meant to belong to a family, and families are meant to show the world, in a small way, something of God's character. Families are part of God's original design![3]

Distribute Bibles and ask someone to read Genesis 2:18-24, and then discuss the following questions:

- What does God say about Adam being alone? (*It isn't good for him.*)
- How does God show Adam that he needs a human companion? (*He causes all the animals to pass in front of Adam, but none of them is suitable as a true helper.*)
- How did God create Eve? (*From Adam's side.*)
- What does being taken from Adam's side show us about Eve's equality with Adam? (*She was taken from his side to be an equal partner and companion. This idea of equality is supported by the fact that the same Hebrew word for "helper" is used in other places in the Old Testament in reference to God Himself—see Exodus 18:4; Deuteronomy 33:29 and Psalm 33:20. Note that the Hebrew word most often translated "rib" [tsela] actually means "side." God didn't just use an insignificant part of the man; He took his whole side and made woman.*)

Transition to a more personal note by explaining that God created a perfect counterpart for man so that men and women together could experience the joy of belonging to a family. Family is all about identity and responsibility. We belong to each other—our identity—and must be committed to each other's success and wellbeing—our responsibility.

To illustrate identity, ask the group what some of the characteristics are that show a person that he or she belongs to a certain family. (*Brown eyes, big noses, dimples, freckles, laugh, and so forth.*) Show students the family photo, pointing out the resemblances. To illustrate responsibility, discuss some of the ways that we can show commitment to our families. (*Serving them, wanting the best for them, helping and supporting their endeavors.*)

Conclude by asking the following questions:

- Is every family a good reflection of God's original plan? (*No, unfortunately many are not.*)
- Does this mean that we should redefine family? (*No, God's Word has already set the standard. We need to come to Him and ask for His grace and help to make our families the kind that can show the world a little of what He's like.*)

Option 2: Stronger Together. For this option, you will need several Bibles, a piece of string, a piece of rope and a globe. Begin by explaining that Genesis is a book of beginnings. Within this book of the Bible, we see the start of all sorts of things, including families. What does the Bible say about families right from the very beginning? (*That we were created to belong together.*)

Distribute Bibles and have students follow along as a volunteer reads Genesis 2:18-24. Continue by stating that after God created Adam, He said that it was not good for man to be alone—that man needed to have someone else to connect with. So God paraded every other animal in the kingdom in front of Adam, just to show Adam that there was no one else like him, no creature that belonged with him. God highlighted his aloneness, but He didn't stop there. God created a counterpart for man, someone like him, so that together they could experience the joy of belonging to a family. From this, we can learn two important points: (1) we have a family on earth, and (2) we have a family in heaven.

First, *we have a family on earth.* Read aloud Psalm 68:6, and then explain that we didn't get to choose our family—God did it for us. We may not always appreciate His choice for our family, but we can trust that He had a reason for the choice He made. God can use our family to bless us and use us to bless them. Ideally, an earthly family is a group of people who encourage and support each other, helping each member to succeed and fulfill God's will.

Now read Ecclesiastes 4:9-12. Continue by stating that we need the help of a family to make it through the challenges of life on a broken planet. To illustrate this, hold up the string and explain that by ourselves we are like this single string, not very strong because it is alone. Hold up the rope and point out the braided single strands that combine to make a single rope, and state that God put us in a family so that we could help, strengthen and encourage each other. Together we are stronger and better able to meet the challenges of life.

We also have a family in heaven. Explain that the ultimate expression of family is found in our heavenly Father. He is the source of true love and care. Make this a visual reality for students by displaying the globe and discussing the wide variety of nations, cultures and people groups that exist today. Emphasize that no matter where they go in the world, the family unit is the primary source of safety, belonging and love.

Read Ephesians 3:14-15 and sum up by stating that family begins and ends with God the Father. In Him we have a parent who accepts us as we are and guides us to become what He wants us to be. God is watching over His children, to help us and direct us every moment of every day.

DIG

Option 1: Where Do I Belong? For this option, you will need this case study. Begin by stating that so far we've talked about God's original design for family, but now we are going to talk about what happens when families don't turn out the way God intended. Read the following case study:

Ever since her mom left, Susan's life had taken a drastic turn. Her dad worked all the time, her little brother had gone to live with their grandmother in another state, and Susan was left alone a lot. Now because her dad's job kept relocating to different cities, she was forced to start all over again in a new school—the third time in less than two years. She desperately wanted to feel like she belonged again, like someone cared about her and had time for her.

During the first few days at the new school, Susan wandered around by herself, trying to figure out where everything was. Finally, she met Troy. He was so friendly and helpful, making sure Susan found all her classes and showing her shortcuts to them. Susan began to feel connected again at last.

After a few weeks, Troy invited Susan to his home. When Susan arrived, she found Troy alone, waiting for her with a six-pack of beer and some R-rated videos. She knew that to go inside would compromise her conscience, but Troy was the only friend she had made, and it felt so good not to be alone.

Now discuss the following questions:

- How is Susan trying to fill the need to belong? (*By searching for someone or something to give her a sense of belonging.*)
- What kinds of social groups exist at your school? (*Help the group to identify the social groups, such as athletes, band members, honor society, special clubs, and so forth.*)

Youth Leader Tip

Whenever you are dealing with issues surrounding the family, it is always good to encourage students to walk in their parents' shoes and think about some of the pressures and struggles that they are facing.[4]

- Why are students attracted to these groups? (*They want to feel a part of something, they enjoy sharing a common interest, they feel stronger because of the friendships they can develop.*)
- When can a social group become a destructive influence on someone? (*When fitting in with the crowd becomes more important than doing what God says is right.*)
- How would a strong family connection have made a difference for Susan in this situation? (*She would not feel so lonely, and her father would probably not allow her to go to the home of a "friend" he did not know. There would be rules to follow in this kind of situation.*)
- What are Susan's options? (*To go ahead and join Troy or to tell him no and leave.*)
- What are some reasons Susan should leave? (*By staying, Susan is opening the door to sin, even though it may seem like an innocent desire for friendship. They are both too young to be drinking beer, seeing R-rated movies and being alone together. She doesn't know Troy or his family very well, and her father doesn't know her whereabouts.*)
- How can realizing God's plan for family help us in daily struggles and choices? (*It helps us know what is right and wrong about relationships. Knowing God's plan can help us see ourselves and others as God sees us and them—as having value and purpose in His plan.*)

Sum up by stating that when families fall apart, the need to belong can be overwhelming and sometimes lead to the sacrifice of conscience—doing what is wrong just to belong. The key to overcoming is to remember that, even when earthly families fail, our heavenly Father is still there, loving and upholding us. Leaning on Him can seem very difficult, but it will bring about the best for us and for those around us.

Option 2: Broken Families. For this option, you just need these questions. Discuss the following with your group:

- If God created families, why are there so many broken ones? (*The answer to this is found in Genesis 3—the fall of man. Adam and Eve's sin affected us all because we inherited a sin nature that leads us to behavior that is selfish and ungodly [see Romans 5:12; 7:5,18]. Sinful people make sinful choices. The good news is that God can redeem any situation and work good in it.*)

- Why do Christians get divorced? (*Sometimes Christians can't seem to get through difficult family problems without giving up and splitting. It is hard work to live with others, and when we leave God out of our relationships, it becomes even more difficult. This doesn't mean that God loves us less or that He will stop trying to bring about His will in our lives. In Philippians 2:13, Paul tells us that God desires nothing but good for everyone, and He will keep working to achieve it.*)

- What if I hate my family and don't want to belong to it? (*Everyone feels frustrated with his or her family from time to time. Realize that families aren't necessarily havens of bliss but are places of growth. The best thing you can do when you can't stand them anymore is to find a way to serve them or think of something that you really do like about them. And you can always pray for them! Ask God for help in difficult relationships.*)

- What if I feel my current family situation is all my fault? (*A child is not responsible for the actions that his or her parents or other adults take. Parents make their own choices. Unfortunately, children often bear the brunt of those hurtful decisions. God doesn't want you to be under condemnation and shame for decisions your parents make. There might be some things you can do, with God's help, to bring more peace and communication to your home.*)

- Has the media caused the breakdown of the family, or does it just reflect a breakdown that would have happened even without its influence? (*Probably a bit of both. Television, movies and music often emphasize non-commitment and easy outs if things get tough. Media also seems to encourage doing or saying hurtful things to others and being selfish. The Bible teaches that we must stick to our word even when it hurts [see Psalm 15:4] and that we must love others as we love ourselves [see Matthew 22:37-39]. By doing so, God is able to bless and honor His Word to us, working things out for His glory, by His grace. If you're looking for what really works, don't get your advice from the tube—get it from God's Word!*)

APPLY

Option 1: Joining God's Family. For this option, you will need your Bible. Ahead of time, mark the following verses for easy reference: Psalm 68:5-6, John 1:12-13, Romans 8:15-16, Galatians 3:26 and 1 John 3:1.

Begin by explaining that there are probably some people in this group who feel completely alone. Their families aren't what they should be, and they feel left out. Tell the group that you want to encourage them today with some verses from God's Word. Read Psalm 68:5-6, and explain that God sets the lonely in families. The first family He wants to set you in is His own. He wants to give you His Spirit and make you His own child.

Now read John 1:12-13. Explain that we can become His children by believing in His name. He will send His Spirit into our hearts, and we will belong to Him. Next, read Romans 8:15-16 and Galatians 3:26. State that being a part of God's family is His gift of grace to you. He loves you so much that He wants to redeem your life and cause you to experience love like you never have before.

Finally, read 1 John 3:1. Ask students to close their eyes and think about the verses you've just read. After a minute, continue by stating that if any of them feel empty inside and know that they are ready to accept God's gift of salvation, they should look up to you. God has provided a way for you to be a part of His family through the cross of Jesus Christ. He shed His blood so that we could be forgiven and brought into His family as His precious child. Make direct eye contact with each student that looks up so that you can follow up with him or her immediately after the session. If possible, have an adult volunteer watch with you to help keep track of those who are receiving Christ.

After you dismiss the session, have those students who looked up meet you in a less noisy area of your room where you can explain more clearly what it means to accept Jesus, and give them Bibles. Get students' names and phone numbers and follow up with them before next week's meeting. You might even send a Welcome to the Family card!

Option 2: Visiting the Lonely. For this option, you will need some inspired ideas from your students.

Use this time to plan a time of ministry to a senior care facility, a hospital ward or an orphanage. Reviewing the Bible verses from this session, have students plan a way to show the love of God for families by serving those who may not be with their families at this time. This could include writing cards, baking cookies, singing and any other act of kindness or service. This might even include visiting a facility together as a group! Once you find the area of your students' greatest enthusiasm, make it happen! Give them the opportunity to show the love of God beyond the four walls of the church. It is a lot of work, but well worth the extra effort.

REFLECT

The following short devotions are for the students to reflect on and answer during the week. You can make a copy of these pages and distribute to your class or download and print from **www.gospellight.com/uncommon/jh_the_old_testament.zip.**

1—BIG FAMILY

Dive into Mark 3:31-35 to see what Jesus says about who belongs to His family.

Wasn't life as a second-grader great? You got to eat snacks at recess, had hardly any homework and had tons more free time. Plus, remember the cool drawings you used to do at school? You drew masterpieces of things such as birds, airplanes, rainbows, flowers and even other people. You even used to draw your family—your parents in the middle and you and your brothers and sisters next to them.

If you were to draw a picture of your whole family today, who do you think God would want you to include? Of course, there's your immediate family: parents and siblings. But then there's the broader family of Christ. Everyone who has a relationship with Jesus is part of God's family—that includes you if you've invited Jesus into your life!

Take a minute to think of three people who are part of your spiritual family that you respect. Thank God for the mentors He has given you and for the members of God's family that help you to grow up spiritually.

2—BECOME A MEMBER

Run to Colossians 3:12-17 to see how to be a member of your church family. What's the purpose of going to church?

- ❑ It gives you a chance to check out cool guys and girls
- ❑ There are fun games and activities that your parents approve of
- ❑ You can hang out with your friends
- ❑ It gives you a chance to grow spiritually with others

Okay, that's really a trick question. All of the above are a part of church, but really the number one purpose for church is to know, worship and proclaim Jesus as Lord, which helps us to grow spiritually with others.

You can study the Bible, pray and even listen to worship music on your own. You can meet guys and girls, play fun games and hang out with friends.

But there's only one place you can go to grow spiritually with others: to a gathering of believers such as you find at church. How much time have you spent lately with your church family members—praying, praising God, studying the Bible or just talking about God?

_____

_____

_____

Do you spend more time making fun of people and cutting people down at church than building them up? Why?

_____

_____

_____

What would you like to do differently the next time you're at church?

_____

_____

_____

Ask God to give you the courage to make some changes and be the kind of person He wants you to be in your church family.

3—WHICH FAMILY DO YOU CHOOSE?

To start things off, read about the Church in Acts 2:42-47.

Imagine a youth group where no one discusses what's *really* going on in their lives. Sure, they talk about movies, the school band or basketball scores, but they don't really talk about their feelings, problems or struggles. And in this group, no one shares what he or she has with anyone else. No one shares clothes or Bibles or even a cell phone to make a phone call. When they get together, all they do is gossip and cut people down.

How is this group different from the one you read about in Acts 2:42-47? Which church family would you rather be a part of?

_____

_____

_____

Okay, that's a pretty easy question, but here's a harder one: What can you do to make your youth group more like the Acts 2 Church?

_____

_____

_____

_____

Who knows, you might just start a landslide of change!

4—SEEKING ADVICE

Read the good news in 1 Corinthians 4:15. When are you most likely to seek out others for advice?

- ❏ When you like a guy or girl and you're not sure what to do
- ❏ When your friends are angry at you and you don't know why
- ❏ When you're failing math and don't know what to tell your parents
- ❏ When your parents are in a big fight and you're scared

Actually, any of these times would be good times to seek advice. God has not just given you earthly parents, but He's given you other wise believers who can help you navigate through the maze of middle school and the rest of life.

What is one thing that you need advice about right now?

_____

_____

_____

_____

Who could you go to for that advice?

_____

_____

_____

_____

When you talk to this person, make sure that you thank him or her for being available and interested in your life!

THE SERPENT: THE BEGINNING OF SIN

THE BIG IDEA

Jesus is the only solution to the problem of sin.

SESSION AIMS

In this session you will guide students to (1) realize that everyone is subject to their own sin nature, which leads to sinful acts; (2) feel encouraged by the power of Jesus' obedience and sacrifice to eradicate sin; and (3) accept God's amazing gift of grace and forgiveness.

THE BIGGEST VERSE

"For just as through the disobedience of the one man the many were made sinners, so also through the obedience of the one man the many will be made righteous" (Romans 5:19).

OTHER IMPORTANT VERSES

Genesis 2:15; 3:1-24; Isaiah 14:12-14; Ezekiel 28:12-17; Matthew 23:27-28; Luke 10:18; Acts 4:12; Romans 3:23,25-26; 5:12; 10:9-10; 14:10-12; 1 Corinthians 10:13; 2 Corinthians 5:17; Galatians 5:16; Ephesians 2:1-2,8-9; 1 Timothy 4:12; Titus 3:5-7; James 1:13-15; 1 John 1:9; Jude 24-25; Revelation 12:9

Note: Additional options and worksheets in 8$^1/_2$" x 11" format for this session are available for download at **www.gospellight.com/uncommon/jh_the_old_testament.zip**.

STARTER

Option 1: S.I.N. For this option, you will need your Bible, a whiteboard and a dry-erase marker. Welcome students and ask if anyone can tell you what an acronym is. (Don't be surprised if no one jumps up and shouts the answer.) Explain that an acronym is a word created from the first letters of a set of words, such as the word "SCUBA," which stands for "Self-Contained Underwater Breathing Apparatus," or "LASER," which stands for "Light Amplification by Stimulated Emission of Radiation." If they are not completely lost by this point, continue by stating that today, we are going to make an acronym in reverse by seeing how many phrases we can create using the letters in the word "sin."

Have the students brainstorm as many acronyms as they can and write these down on the whiteboard. Explain to the group that they don't have to be serious but they should reflect in some way the meaning of the original word. A couple of suggestions to get them started might be: "Some Icky Nonsense" or "Stupid Ignorant Naughtiness." (You get the point, right?)

Allow for as many suggestions as you can fit on the whiteboard. Next, state something like the following: "We can all agree that sin isn't a good thing, right? In fact, the Bible uses many words to describe sin: 'unrighteousness,' 'injustice,' 'corruption,' 'evil,' 'transgression,' 'lawlessness,' 'godlessness,' 'disobedience,' and more. But did you know that sin literally means to miss the mark or to fall short of the goal? And no matter how much we try to avoid it, we all sin every day of our lives. If God created a perfect world, how is this possible?"

Conclude by stating that today we're going to discover how sin began, how it affects us and what God did about it.

Option 2: Wheel of Misfortune. For this option, you will need an adult volunteer, one die (that's the singular form of "dice," in case you didn't already realize it), a whiteboard, a dry-erase marker and a prize for everyone.

Ahead of time, prepare for a game of Wheel of Misfortune by drawing a horizontal line on the whiteboard for each letter of the following phrase, leaving a space between words: "For all have sinned and fall short of the glory of God" (Romans 3:23). Make sure that you *don't write the Bible reference!* (*Note:* if you would like to play several rounds, use other Bible verses or common phrases *first,* and then end with Romans 3:23.)

Divide students into four teams and ask each team to designate a member to play Wheel of Misfortune. Have the four team representatives come forward. Explain that when it is each one's turn, he or she will toss the die to see how many points will be awarded for each consonant in the phrase that is guessed correctly. For instance, if someone rolls a five and correctly guesses a letter in the phrase (consonants only), he or she will get five points for each time the letter appears in the phrase. If the consonant is not in the phrase, the turn goes to the next contestant. However, contestants must give up five points to guess a vowel. If the vowel guessed is in the phrase, the contestant will earn 10 points and continue to guess; if the vowel guessed is *not* in the phrase, he loses five points *and* his turn. A contestant can use her turn to solve the puzzle and guess the phrase, but if she guesses incorrectly, she is out of the game.

Allow the contestant on your far left to roll the die and begin the game. Have the adult volunteer keep a running total of credits and debits for the contestants, and when the phrase is finally guessed, applaud the winning team and announce all the teams' total points. Distribute the prizes. Explain that while some of them might think that only the winning team deserves the prize (after all, the other teams lost, right?), as we'll see today, just like the verse Romans 3:23 teaches, we're all alike in that we sin (meaning we miss the mark) and we need God to help us.

MESSAGE

Option 1: The Stain of Sin. For this option, you will need several Bibles, food coloring and a clear glass pitcher of water.

Begin by explaining that we've been talking about the beginning of things like the world, people and families. But how did sin begin? How did a perfect world get all messed up? Distribute Bibles and have students read Genesis 3. You can do this by passing off verses (each student reads two verses and then calls out the name of someone else to continue) or by going around the group in order. Allow students to decline if they feel uncomfortable reading aloud.

After the chapter has been read, discuss the following questions:

- Who was this serpent? (*The serpent was Satan, who used to be a high-ranking angel in heaven named Lucifer [see Isaiah 14:12-14; Ezekiel 28:12-17; Luke 10:18; Revelation 12:9]. "Lucifer" is the Latin translation of the words "morning star," referred to in Isaiah 14:12.)*
- How did a serpent get into the garden? (*In Genesis 2:15, Adam had been given the job of watching over the garden. Rather than sound the alarm at the serpent's arrival, Adam allowed it to enter.)*
- What is temptation? (*Feeling torn between whether to choose God's way or your own way; see James 1:14-15.)*

- Why did Eve and Adam give in to the temptation? (*Satan deceived Eve, and then they both decided that the serpent was right—that God's Word wasn't the final authority. They chose their will over God's.*)
- What was the result of Adam and Eve's disobedience? (*They were separated from their relationship with God and forced to leave the garden.*)[1]

Read Romans 5:12 and Ephesians 2:1-2 aloud, and then ask the following:

- Why are we tempted? (*When Adam and Eve disobeyed God, sin entered the world and took captive every person that would ever be born.*)
- What is some evidence that all people have a sin nature? (*People never have to be taught to disobey; they do it all on their own because their hearts are inclined toward it. This is the sin nature in all of us.*)

To illustrate this last point, show the glass pitcher of water and put in several drops of food coloring. Explain that the food coloring represents Adam and Eve's original sin and the rest of the water represents all of humankind. Point out that just as the dye stains the water, their sin contaminated every human being born after them. Now continue by discussing the following:

- What do you think is at the root of all sin? (*Pride—thinking our way is better than God's.*)
- Did Adam and Eve realize the consequences their disobedience would have not only on themselves but also on others? (*Probably not.*)
- Do we realize the consequences our disobedience has on others? (*Again, probably not. Temptation causes us to become shortsighted. It presses us to do what will benefit us at the moment, without thinking much about the effect it will have on others.*)
- What was God's response to this heartbreaking event? (*He still loved all humankind. He began to make a way for them—and for us—to be brought back to that close relationship He designed for them to experience. Genesis 3:21 tells us that He made garments out of animal skins for Adam and Eve, symbolizing the blood sacrifice and the covering we would receive as His grace would come to us in the Person of Jesus Christ.*)

Option 2: Just One Bite. For this option, you will need an apple for each student, several nails, one or more magnets and paper clips.

Begin by explaining that God made Adam and Eve and placed them in the garden to care for it. Give each student an apple to eat as you bring this familiar Bible story to life through an unprecedented dramatic reading of Adam and Eve's temptation and fall, from Genesis 3:1-24. (Well, just give it your best shot!) Ask the group to notice the process of temptation to sin described here:

1. The serpent *cast doubt* on God's Word: "Did God really say . . . ?" (verse 1).
2. Eve *added* to God's Word: "and you must not touch it" (verse 3).
3. Satan *contradicted* God's Word: "You will not surely die . . . you will be like God" (verses 4-5).
4. Satan *cast doubt* on God's character: "For God knows . . . your eyes will be opened" (verse 5).
5. Eve *disobeyed* God's Word: "she took some and ate it" (verse 6).
6. Adam *disobeyed* God's Word: "and he ate it" (verse 6).

Explain that Adam and Eve knew God's Word, but they chose to follow their own will instead. They asserted their independence from God by choosing their will over His. As a result, they would no longer enjoy God's presence in the garden. They were kicked out and had to live under the cursed condition that existed in the world outside of God's perfect plan.

Illustrate this by doing the following experiment. Hold up the nail and state that a regular, ordinary nail like this won't attract anything to itself. Try to pick up the paper clip. Now begin to stroke the *nail in one direction* across the magnet. State that when the nail comes into contact with a magnet, however, it changes. (It will take about 50 *strokes in the same direction*, but eventually the nail will become a temporary magnet.) Use the nail, which represents Adam and Eve, to pick up a paper clip, which symbolizes sin. Explain that this nail is just like Adam and Eve. When God first created them, they weren't drawn to sin. After they disobeyed, however, their hearts became corrupted by sin.

Continue by stating that this sin nature was passed on to every person ever born on this earth. We are now naturally drawn to do the wrong things. We have all been magnetized toward sin. At this point, if you have time, invite several students to magnetize a nail as a reminder of the way they are also attracted toward sin. (Make sure they're well supervised when they do this!)

Conclude by stating that we were created by God to enjoy a relationship with Him, but through our rebellion we turn away to live the way we think is best by doubting, adding to or contradicting God's Word. Our hearts yield to little sins because of the sin nature that prevails in us. Just like the nail and the paper clip. Uplifting, huh? Well, the good news is that God never stopped loving

Adam and Eve, and He never stops loving us—even when we sin. His grace is stronger than any sin and can bring our hearts back to His own.

DIG

Option 1: Clean Slate. For this option, you will need a magic slate (you know, those little boards with a black cardboard slate that is covered with an acetate sheet that, when lifted, erases whatever was written on it).

Begin by discussing the following questions:

- What do people do to try to get rid of the sin in their lives? (*Let students come up with suggestions, but summarize using three categories—good works, denial and religion—and write them on the magic slate.*)

- What are some good works that you think would impress God? (*Feeding hungry people, visiting the elderly in rest homes, giving money to charities, obeying the Ten Commandments, and so forth.*)

Read Ephesians 2:8-9 and Titus 3:5-7 and discuss why good works do not get rid of sin. (*Good works don't change our sinful nature.*) Explain that only grace can change our hearts and restore our fellowship with God. This grace is given through Jesus Christ to all who believe. We can never be good enough to earn forgiveness. Now continue by asking the following:

- How do people deny their sin? (*By saying there is no such thing as sin or by rationalizing it through relativism, which is the belief that any belief system is okay as long as you really believe it.*)

- Does denying sin make it go away? (*No. According to Romans 14:10-12, all of us will be held accountable when we stand before God.*)

- What about religion? Can it offer forgiveness? (*Belonging to a church, mosque or temple won't get rid of the sin in your life. Think about the Pharisees of Jesus' day. They were extremely religious, yet in Matthew 23:27-28 Jesus called them whitewashed tombs, which means they looked okay on the outside, but on the inside they were decaying and rotten! Religion in and of itself can do nothing to change our hearts.*)

- Thinking about these three choices, which of these ways have you tried to get rid of sin? (*Give the group a moment for reflection.*)

Now lift the covering of the magic slate and erase the words. Explain that good works, denial or religion cannot offer a solution to the problem of our sin nature. The Bible tells us that only when we pursue a changed heart through a relationship with Jesus Christ can we experience true freedom from sin.

Option 2: Born as Brats! For this option, you need your Bible and this book! Read aloud the following case study:

Dawn dreaded baby-sitting for the Davis family. Although Mr. and Mrs. Davis and their three-year-old daughter were really nice, their two-year-old son, Kelly, was another story. No matter what Dawn did, Kelly didn't like it. He refused to share his toys with his sister and threw a temper tantrum whenever Dawn made him stop playing and tried to get him ready for bed. One morning after baby-sitting for them, Dawn comes to you between your first and second class and shares how awful it went for her last night. She explains, "I don't get it—how can a two-year-old be such a brat?"

Now discuss the following questions:

- What answer could you give that would include some of what we've learned from Genesis 3? (*Selfish behavior is living proof of our fallen nature. You don't have to teach kids to be selfish—it comes naturally!*)
- What exactly is a sin nature? (*A sin nature is having thoughts and desires that are bent toward evil. That means, given the opportunity, we will choose to do what is wrong, because we are bent in that direction.*)
- Can obeying rules change our sin nature? (*No, it might stop unwanted behavior for a while, but eventually, we will stumble into sin again.*)
- How can we get rid of this bent toward sin? (*We need the change of heart that only comes from experiencing spiritual rebirth; see Titus 3:5-7 and 2 Corinthians 5:17.*)
- What advice would you give Dawn for her next baby-sitting adventure? (*Bring some duct tape. Just kidding!*)

APPLY

Option 1: Take the Elevator. For this option, you will need time to pray. Oh, and yes, your Bible, gift Bibles and a ladder.

Conclude this session with an opportunity for students to receive the gift of grace that you've been talking about the whole session. Show the group the ladder and explain that a lot of times, we try on our own to somehow reach God—we try to climb the ladder to Him. Because of our sin, that's impossible. God knows that and has given us an alternative: Jesus! Jesus becomes like our elevator that allows us to overcome our sin and have a close relationship with God.

Have everyone close his or her eyes. State that maybe they've never really understood how to get rid of the sin in their lives. Maybe they thought that just being good was enough, and now they realize that it isn't. Today, you want to give them the opportunity to pray with you right now to receive new life and forgiveness.

Read Romans 10:9-10 and Acts 4:12 aloud. Continue by stating that the Bible makes it clear that forgiveness and salvation are given to us through faith in Jesus Christ. It's not what we can do, but what He *did* that allows such amazing grace to come our way. If anyone present would like to open their heart to His lordship, turning away from their own way to follow His, they should look up at you right now.

After making eye contact with students, lead them in a prayer of repentance, and then close by reading Jude 24-25 as a prayer of praise for God's marvelous gift! Be sure to make contact after the meeting with each student who prayed with you.[2]

Option 2: Resisting Temptation. For this option, you will need copies of "Resisting Temptation Journal" (found on the next page).

Distribute "Resisting Temptation Journal" and point out that the handout has seven days' worth of journal entries. Instruct students to take them home and for the next week record at least one temptation to sin that they overcame each day. Explain that no one is immune to temptation; we all face it every single day of our lives. The key to resisting temptation is to start recognizing it. Once we recognize it, we can resist it by taking it to God in prayer and asking Him to strengthen us. When you use this handout as a reminder to watch out for temptation, you'll be surprised at your ability to recognize it this week—and how many times it creeps into your life!

Close in prayer, asking God to create an awareness in students of temptations in the coming week and to show them the difference that resisting temptations can make in their lives.

Resisting Temptation Journal

So I say, live by the Spirit, and you will not gratify the desires of the sinful nature.
Galatians 5:16

Day 1
Today I resisted the temptation to _____

Possible consequences of giving in to the temptation: _____

_____

Day 2
Today I resisted the temptation to _____

Possible consequences of giving in to the temptation: _____

_____

Day 3
Today I resisted the temptation to _____

Possible consequences of giving in to the temptation: _____

_____

Day 4
Today I resisted the temptation to _____

Possible consequences of giving in to the temptation: _____

_____

Day 5
Today I resisted the temptation to _____

Possible consequences of giving in to the temptation: _____

_____

Day 6
Today I resisted the temptation to _____

Possible consequences of giving in to the temptation: _____

_____

Day 7
Today I resisted the temptation to _____

Possible consequences of giving in to the temptation: _____

_____

REFLECT

The following short devotions are for the students to reflect on and answer during the week. You can make a copy of these pages and distribute to your class or download and print from **www.gospellight.com/uncommon/jh_ the_old_testament.zip.**

1—WHAT'S THAT SMELL?

Read Matthew 23:25-28 for a description of something even worse than terrible bad breath.

Bad breath stinks! Some people have a condition called halitosis—a.k.a. chronic bad breath. No matter how many Tic Tacs these people eat or how many times they brush their teeth, they just can't get rid of their bad breath. Sometimes the cause of halitosis, though, is not in the mouth. Halitosis can actually be caused by problems in the stomach or in the intestines.

How are the teachers of the law and Pharisees similar to people who suffer from halitosis?

_____

_____

_____

_____

What is the solution to their problem, according to Jesus?

_____

_____

_____

How do you try to mask, or cover up, sin in your life?

_____

_____

_____

_____

Rather than masking your sin, you can turn to Jesus and ask Him to take away your sin. He is the only one who can clean you from the inside out. Ask Him to help you make good choices and resist temptations today.

2—GOOD VS. EVIL

What does God say about our ability to be good on our own? To find out, read Psalm 14:2-3.

Is humankind basically good or basically evil? I dare you to ask three of your friends this question. My guess is that they will answer, "Basically good." Our culture today and many psychologists tell us that people are basically good at heart but become bad because of their surroundings, or their environment. But does the Bible agree that people are basically good?

What does Psalm 14:2-3 say in regard to the basically good/basically evil question?

_____

_____

_____

The good news is that because of Jesus, we have power over sin. Spend some time thanking Jesus for overcoming sin in your life, and ask Him to help you resist specific temptations today.

3—STAY TUNED

Choose to read Romans 8:5-11 to see what Paul says about the effect of our choices.

Where is your mindset today? Televisions and radios can only pick up the station that they are tuned to. That's kind of similar to how our minds work. You have a choice to make, today and every day. Will you tune in to God's Spirit, allowing Him to work in you to transform and reform you into the image of Christ, or will you tune in to your sin nature, continuing to conform to the world?

What are some ways that you can make sure your mind is set on what the Spirit desires, today and every day?

_____

_____

_____

Try out whatever you come up with! Thank Jesus today for being at work in you and changing you from the inside out.

4—A BAD APPLE

Read Micah 7:18-19 to see what God does with our sins.

Have you ever eaten an apple that is rotten but didn't realize it was rotten until you got to the core? At its deepest core, sin is self-centeredness—each of us wanting to do our own thing at any cost. Sin, like a rotten apple, looks good on the outside, but on the inside it is spoiled.

Our self-centeredness and sin ultimately build a high wall that separates us from God and other people. But thankfully, we have a merciful God who comes to us even in our self-centeredness and breaks down the wall and brings us into new relationships with Himself and with others.

Rewrite Micah 7:18-19 in your own words.

_____

_____

_____

_____

What difference would it make in your life if you really believed these verses and lived according to that belief today?

_____

_____

_____

_____

Ask God to help you live out His Word in a new way today.

NOAH: THE BEGINNING OF WORSHIP

THE BIG IDEA

Worship was designed by God for us to recognize and appreciate the unique relationship we have with Him.

SESSION AIMS

In this session you will guide students to (1) realize that God initiated covenant relationship with them; (2) feel grateful for who God is and what He has done for them; and (3) respond with life choices that worship their Redeemer and God: Jesus.

THE BIGGEST VERSE

"I will remember my covenant between me and you and all living creatures of every kind" (Genesis 9:15).

OTHER IMPORTANT VERSES

Genesis 6:1–9:17; Psalm 115:8; Luke 19:10; Ephesians 4:25,29; 5:19; Philippians 2:13; 4:8; Colossians 3:17; 1 Peter 3:10-12; 1 John 4:10; Revelation 21:1

Note: Additional options and worksheets in 8$^1/_2$" x 11" format for this session are available for download at **www.gospellight.com/uncommon/jh_the_old_testament.zip**.

STARTER

Option 1: How Much Is It Worth? For this option, you will need three identical sets of five different objects, each object of different value (for example: a marble, a six pack of soda, a music CD, a T-shirt and a concert ticket), three paper grocery bags and a long table. Ahead of time, set up the table at the front of the room and put the three bags on the table, with one set of objects inside each bag.

Greet students and remind them that the theme of Genesis is beginnings. Ask what they remember most from the previous lessons about the beginning of creation, family and sin. Then introduce today's topic: the beginning of worship.

Ask three volunteers to come forward and give each volunteer a bag containing one set of the five objects. At your signal, have volunteers put the objects on the table, facing the group, in order based on what the value of each item is to them, from the highest value to the lowest. After they have finished, go through the objects and ask the volunteers why they ordered them the way they did (for instance, why was the CD worth more than the marble?). Be sure to highlight any differences in what the students valued most.

Sum up by explaining that sometimes things are obviously more valuable than others, but sometimes it depends on personal choice. For example, depending on if you like the CD or not or how many T-shirts you have, you might have chosen one over the other while someone else might have placed them in a different order. However, one thing is certain—whenever we acknowledge the value of something, we are acknowledging what that thing is worth.

Transition by stating that today we are going to look at the beginning of worship. Explain to the group that the word "worship" comes from the old English word *worthship,* which means to recognize the worth or value that something or someone has.[1] When we worship God, we are saying that we value Him—who He is and what He has done for us. We are saying that He is worth something to us. In worship we aren't deciding how much God is

Youth Leader Tip

Always review your last session before moving on to new territory. If your sessions build on each other, your students will gain biblical knowledge and understanding that will help them see how all the pieces fit together.

worth or how valuable He is; instead, we are responding to His revelation of His intrinsic worth and majesty. As we'll see today, worship is much more than merely singing songs; it is acknowledging the One who is worthy of all praise and honor—God!

Option 2: Name that Price. For this option, you will need several small index cards, pens or pencils, prizes, three items for a price-guessing game (somewhat unusual items, like round-trip bus tickets to Des Moines, a box of detergent, a desk lamp, and so on), a table for displaying the items and a sheet to cover them. Ahead of time, for each item, write its actual retail price on an index card and place the card face down in front of the item displayed.

Select three volunteers who think they're pretty good at guessing the price of items. Have them come forward and stand in front of the display (which should be covered) and distribute three index cards and a pen or pencil to each contestant. Explain that each time you uncover an item, the contestants are to write on one of their cards their estimated price for the item. Allow 10 seconds for students to figure out their bids, and then call on each of the contestants to hold up their cards and read his or her estimate out loud. Turn over the item's price and award a prize to the contestant who comes closest to the actual price *without going over*. For instance, let's say an item retails for $28.99. Samantha bids $31.00, Jorge bids $30.00, and Ryan bids $25.00. Ryan wins that round because he came closest without bidding over the real price.

Explain that everything has value, but some things are more valuable than others. Value can be placed because of a monetary cost—a Lamborghini costs much more than a Ford Mustang—or it can be because a particular item has a personal meaning for someone. You might value a necklace because your grandmother gave it to you. There is one thing we should value the most, though, regardless of who we are, and it's been given to us for *free*: it's our relationship with God. God has provided everything on this earth, including the things we value. Our relationship with Him—our worship of Him—should reflect our gratitude for who He is and what He has done for us.

MESSAGE

Option 1: Noah Trivia. For this option, you will need your Bible (but then again, don't we always?).

Begin by stating that now that we know what worship is, we will look at a man who worshiped God with his whole life: Noah. Many of your students will probably think they already know everything there is to know about the story of Noah from the Bible, so do a quick game of True or False to check their knowledge levels. Have students respond to the following questions by standing up if they think the answer is true and sitting down if they think it's false. As you answer each question, be sure to read the corresponding Bible reference.

- God was so disappointed with the world and its inhabitants that He decided to scrap it and start all over again. (*True. The people of Noah's day didn't care at all about God or His ways. According to Genesis 6:5-14, God was so grieved over man's wickedness and unwillingness to repent that He had no choice but to let the judgment upon sin run its course. God's justice cannot ignore sin forever, or He wouldn't be just. Sin will lead to misery and death unless human repentance invites God's mercy to intervene.*)

- Noah found out about God's plan and begged to be spared. (*False. Genesis 6:8-9 states that God came to Noah because He saw that Noah was the only man on the whole earth living a blameless and upright life. This emphasizes the incredible grace of God—that He initiates a relationship with us; see also Luke 19:10; 1 John 4:10.*)

- Noah was a widower with five small children. (*False. Genesis 6:10 states that Noah had a wife and three sons.*)

- God told Noah to build an ark that was one and a half football fields long and as tall as a five-story building. (*True. The dimensions of the ark were 450 feet long, 75 feet wide and 45 feet tall; see Genesis 6:15.*)

- God told Noah to bring two of every kind of animal into the ark. (*False. Genesis 7:2-3 states that God told Noah to bring two of every kind of unclean animal and seven of every kind of clean animal and bird.*)

- As soon as Noah shut the door of the ark, it started to rain. (*False. First, God shut the door of the ark Himself [see Genesis 7:16]. Second, the rain didn't begin for seven more days [see Genesis 7:4,7-10].*)

- It rained nonstop for 40 days and 40 nights. (*True. According to Genesis 7:17-20, the rain was so intense that the top of every mountain on earth was covered by 20 feet of water.*)

- After 40 days, Noah and his family and all the animals came out of the ark. (*False. It took over a year for all the water to dry up so that they could leave the ark—compare Genesis 7:11 with 8:13-14.*)

- Noah knew there was dry ground because he sent out a dove who returned with an olive branch in its beak. (*True. Genesis 8:8-12 states that the first time the dove was sent out it couldn't find a place to land; the second time it came back with an olive branch; the third time it didn't return.*)

- The first thing Noah did when he got off the ark was kiss the ground. (*False. Well, he might have done that too, but the Bible tells us that Noah built an altar to worship God—see Genesis 8:20.*)

- God swore He would never destroy the earth again. (*False. In Genesis 9:11, God promised to never destroy the earth with a flood again. Scripture tells us that eventually the earth will be destroyed [see 2 Peter 3:10-12] and God will create a new one in its place [see Revelation 21:1].*)

- God set a rainbow in the sky as a sign of His promise not to destroy the earth and its inhabitants with a flood. (*True. God established a covenant with Noah that ensured blessing and protection. This offered mankind a unique relationship to God—a covenant relationship between the Creator and all mankind [see Genesis 9:12-17].*)

Have everyone sit down, and then explain that the story of Noah shows us more than how God saved one family from a flood; it points out a very important part of our relationship with God—a *covenant*. A covenant is an agreement between two parties, obligating them both to certain specific terms. For instance, a marriage is a covenant between a man and a woman to love and faithfully live with each other until they die.

Continue by stating that human covenants sometimes fail, but God's do not. God, in His grace, made a covenant with humankind that will never fail. The terms of His covenant with us are this: He offers salvation and eternal life, and we accept His gracious gift. As a result, we are to live in a way that reflects gratitude for who He is and what He's done—we worship Him. And the best part is that He will help us do this (see Philippians 2:13)! Make this personal by explaining that while the rest of the world allowed itself to be ruled by selfish desires, Noah worshiped God by leading a life of obedience and submission to Him. More than anything, Noah wanted to please God.

Conclude by stating that when we live in intense gratefulness and faith-driven obedience to God and His Word, we are declaring that we value Him and that we want to worship Him in all we say, think and do.

Option 2: Flood Drama. For this option, you will need several Bibles and prizes. Ahead of time, select several key verses from Genesis 6:1–9:17 (some suggestions include 6:6; 6:14; 7:13; 7:24; 8:13; 8:20; 9:12).

Divide students into groups of three to five each. Assign each group one or more of the verses you've chosen ahead of time and send them off for five minutes to figure out how they would act out the verse(s) that they've been given. In random order, ask each group to act out their assigned verse(s), one at a time. The rest of the groups will compete to try to figure out what is going on in the drama and then find where in Genesis 6:1–9:17 it is located. Keep track of which group finds the most verses first, and reward that group with a prize.

Next, explain that everything we do in our lives—every choice we make— gives us an opportunity to worship God. Worship isn't just singing and praising Him; it's living according to His will for our lives. Read Genesis 6:9 and explain that while Noah wasn't perfect, he did try in every area of his life to please God. His godly life was a huge contrast to the wickedness of the rest of mankind, and he was rewarded for his faithfulness. Now discuss the following questions:

- How would you have felt if you had been Noah? (*Probably a little fearful and alone, but also excited.*)
- What do you think your friends would say about you as you were building such an enormous boat? (*You're crazy; you're out of your mind; God never spoke to you; and so on.*)
- How would you try to explain the project to them? (*God told you to do it, and as His servant, you are being obedient to His word.*)
- In Genesis 7, God instructed Noah and his family to go into the ark and take animals with them. But then seven days went by without rain. How would you have felt if you were Noah during this time? (*Anxious, but trusting in the Lord.*)
- What about when it started raining? How would you have felt stuck in a boat with all those animals? (*Again, anxious, but trusting in the Lord.*)
- In Genesis 8:20, we read Noah's response after he leaves the ark. How does this relate to worship? (*Noah's first priority was to give God thanks for bringing him and his family safely through the flood.*)
- In Genesis 8:21, we read that this act was "pleasing" to God. Why do you think this was the case? (*Noah could have gotten his family settled, unloaded the ark and built a house, but instead, he honored God first through a worship sacrifice.*)

DIG

Option 1: Worship Choices. For this option, you will need several Bibles, worship music, a way to play the music, and copies of "Worship Choices" (found on the next page) and pens or pencils.

Distribute Bibles, "Worship Choices" and pens or pencils and instruct students to look up and write out each Scripture reference. This can be done individually or in small groups, depending on the maturity of the group. Use the worship music as background music for the study time. After everyone is finished, regroup and discuss the following questions:

- How can we worship God with our words? (*By only speaking what will encourage and help others; using words that honor and exalt Him; singing or speaking praise. Read Ephesians 4:25 and 5:19 and give an example of a time when you did this.*)

- How can we worship God with our thoughts? (*By thinking on things that are good and pure, meditating on His Word, having an attitude of thankfulness. Read Philippians 4:8 and give an example of a time when you did this.*)

- How can we worship God with our actions? (*Living in obedience to His Word; doing things that are kind and helpful, even when others won't say thank you or will even know about it; being honest and truthful. Read Colossians 3:17 and give an example of a time when you did this.*)

Sum up by stating that every choice we make honors someone—either ourselves, someone else or God. By choosing to honor Him in our words, thoughts and actions, we are showing Him how much He means to us.

Option 2: Give Your Best. For this option, you won't need a thing except this book. Explain that every day our choices do one of two things: they honor God or they don't. Sounds simple, doesn't it? What about the choices we make that don't have an impact on anyone else? Do those choices count? Read the following case study:

Long ago, a band of musicians lived in a faraway land. They traveled from town to town, singing and playing their music. Times were hard and the common people had little money to spend on luxuries like concerts, even though the musicians didn't charge much at all.

WORSHIP
CHOICES

We worship God with our **words** (Ephesians 4:29; 5:19)

_____
_____
_____
_____
_____
_____

We worship God with our **thoughts** (Philippians 4:8)

_____
_____
_____
_____
_____
_____

We worship God with our **actions** (Colossians 3:17)

_____
_____
_____
_____
_____

The group met one evening to discuss their dreary plight. "I see no reason to play tonight," said one. "It's snowing, and no one will come out on a night like this."

Another said, "I agree. Last night there were only a handful of people; surely even fewer will come tonight."

The leader of the troupe responded, "I know you are discouraged. I am, too. But we have a responsibility to those who *do* come. We will play tonight as planned and we will play our best to honor our guests. Those that come deserve nothing less."

Encouraged by his words, the musicians gave their best performance ever that night. After the show, the leader called to his troupe. He slowly read aloud a note he had received from an audience member just as the curtain fell after the performance. The note read, "Thank you for a beautiful performance," and was signed simply, "Your King."[2]

Now discuss the following questions:

- Why did the king send a thank-you note to the musicians? (*He was honored at their heartfelt efforts to share their music.*)
- What might have happened if the musicians had cancelled their show? (*The king—and everyone else who attended—might have felt discouraged that his presence at the concert wasn't enough for them to play.*)
- How does this relate to the decisions we make, even when it seems like those decisions wouldn't really affect anyone else? (*Every decision we have to make is an opportunity to honor God and to say thank you to Him for all He has done for us.*)

Explain that God is honored when we seek to do our best and to please Him, regardless of who might be looking. Every time we choose to follow God's will and do our best for Him, we are worshiping Him.

APPLY

Option 1: My Reflection. For this option, you will need note paper, pens or pencils, small mirrors and paint pens (which can be purchased at office supply or craft stores).

Begin by discussing some of the characteristics of God. What is He like? (*Peaceful, forgiving, merciful, loving, strong, wise, patient—the list goes on and on.*)

Continue by stating that Psalm 115:8 says we become like the thing or person we worship. Distribute the mirrors and have students look at their reflections.

Continuing by explaining that when we look in the mirror, we need to ask ourselves whose character we want to reflect. By worshiping God, we will be shaped more and more into His likeness. This doesn't mean that we can *become* God, but we can become *like* Him, just as a child is like his parent(s). The more we become like Him, the more others around us will see His love and want to know Him, too. (*Note*: This would be an ideal time to extend an invitation for students to accept Christ as their Lord and Savior if you feel it is appropriate. Be sensitive to the group and challenge them with a question or two about the authenticity of their faith. How can they really worship God unless they've come into a relationship with Him?)

Distribute paper and pens or pencils and invite students to write down the characteristics of God that they would like to have Him develop in their own lives as they worship Him. Distribute the paint pens and invite students to rewrite the characteristics on the mirror around the outside edges, like a border.

End in prayer, thanking God for His goodness and His desire to make us like Him. Ask Him to provide opportunities every day for students to worship Him and become more like Him.

Option 2: I'll Remember. For this option, you will need copies of "I'll Remember" (found on the next page) and pens or pencils. Begin by explaining that God isn't just interested in *us;* He is interested in everyone around us as well. Just as He had Noah bring his family into the ark, He also wants *us* to bring everyone we can into His presence.

Distribute "I'll Remember" and pens or pencils and ask students to write down the names of everyone in their immediate families (whether or not they already know God) across the rainbow. Pair them off and have each student pray for his or her partner's family members by name, asking for God's blessing to come to them. When the pairs have prayed for the members listed in each family, have them switch partners and pray with someone else.

Suggest that students take their papers home and place them somewhere where they'll see them during the week, to remind them to continue to pray for God's power to be shown in their family's lives and to remind them to worship God with their own lives during the upcoming week.[3]

i'll remember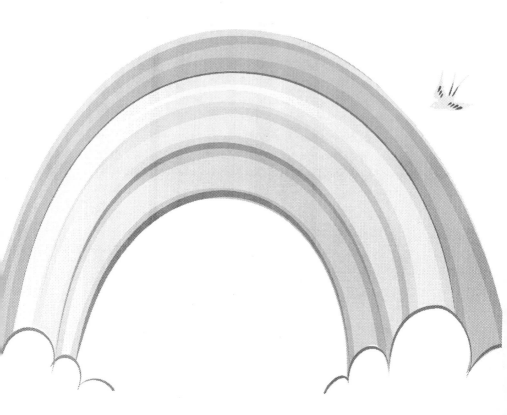

"I will remember my covenant between me and you."
Genesis 9:15

REFLECT

The following short devotions are for the students to reflect on and answer during the week. You can make a copy of these pages and distribute to your class or download and print from **www.gospellight.com/uncommon/jh_the_old_testament.zip**.

1—THE PSALM SONGBOOK

Did you know that the book of Psalms in the Bible was actually ancient Israel's songbook? They sang these psalms when they worshiped!

Read Psalm 100 and put it to music (either a secular or a Christian song) that would help you memorize it. After reading this psalm, what does it tell you about how you should worship God? Put a checkmark in any box where the sentence is true.

- ❑ We should be joyful and upbeat when we worship God.
- ❑ We should always worship God in a serious and quiet manner.
- ❑ We should worship God because He is good, faithful and loving.
- ❑ We should worship God with more than just singing.
- ❑ We can only worship God when we are in a good mood.

You should have checked all of the above answers except for "we should always worship God in a serious and quiet manner" and "we can only worship God when we are in a good mood." Did you get them all correct? If not, what does that tell you about your view of worship?

_____

_____

_____

_____

How can you change that?

_____

_____

_____

Ask God to show you His truth about worship and help you model that truth for others.

2—WORSHIP ANYTIME

Do a little eavesdropping and read John 4:19-24, the tail end of a conversation that Jesus had with a Samaritan woman He met at a well.

When you hear the word "sleep," what is the first thing you think of? Chances are, you think of your own room and your own bed. But have you—or someone you know—ever fallen asleep in class? It is so funny to watch others fall asleep, but it can be pretty embarrassing for those who are doing the sleeping (and sometimes snoring or drooling as well) in class. Needless to say, even though the best place to fall asleep is in the comfort of your own warm bed, you could actually fall asleep just about anywhere.

In the same way, when you hear the word "worship," what is the first thing you think of? Chances are, you think of your church or of the time you spend singing there. But worship doesn't just happen at church, and it doesn't just happen when you sing. Worship can (and should) happen anywhere!

According to Jesus, what is more important than the place where we worship?

_____

_____

_____

What are two ways you can worship God, other than singing?

_____

_____

_____

Where could you worship Him today?

_____

_____

3—CHECK YOUR ATTITUDE

Read Isaiah 1:11-17 to find that when it comes to worshiping God, what really matters is our attitude on the inside!

Sometimes, I love to go to church, thought Jonathon. *But other times, I don't even know why I'm there! And I hate it when my parents make me go, but at least then I can talk to my friends.*

Going to church is an important part of how we worship God. It's not all we can do to worship God and grow in our relationship with Him, but it is an important way we can worship and grow.

Ancient Israel also had an important tradition that God asked them to do as a way of worshiping Him: sacrificing animals. This was the way they could gain access to God and express on the outside their love and dependence on Him. (Later God sent Jesus, the final sacrifice, and ended what is called the sacrificial system.) But what really matters is not what people do on the outside! Jonathon goes to church, but when he has a bad attitude, going to church becomes less meaningful.

Spend some time in prayer, asking God to rekindle your love for Him so you can show your thankfulness to Him by your lifestyle and good attitude.

4—WHAT HAVE YOU DONE FOR HIM LATELY?

Run to Romans 12:1-2 to find out what you can do for God.

Way back in the 1980s, Janet Jackson came out with a song called "What Have You Done for Me Lately?" This song is basically telling a friend, "I'm not going to be doing anything for you because you haven't done anything for me lately." But God has done a really wonderful thing for us in paying for our sins and bringing us into a relationship with Him through Christ. God did not first ask, "What have you done for me lately?" He simply acted with mercy toward us out of His incredible love for us. We should be asking ourselves, *What have I done for Him lately?*

According to Romans 12:1-2, how can we respond to God in order to show how thankful we are to Him?

_____

_____

_____

_____

What do you think it means to offer your body as a living sacrifice to God?

_____

_____

_____

_____

ABRAHAM:
THE BEGINNING
OF FAITH

THE BIG IDEA

Our relationship with God is based upon and sustained by faith.

SESSION AIMS

In this session you will guide students to (1) understand that they can relate to God only through faith; (2) deepen their faith in God by recapturing the amazing grace given in Christ Jesus; and (3) choose one way to express their faith this week.

THE BIGGEST VERSE

"Abraham believed God, and it was credited to him as righteousness" (Romans 4:3).

OTHER IMPORTANT VERSES

Genesis 12:1-5; 15:1-6; 21:1-3; 22:1-18; Exodus 15:26; Numbers 23:19; Nehemiah 9:31; Psalm 145; Proverbs 3:5-6; Jeremiah 32:17; Matthew 19:26; John 11:25; Acts 4:12; Romans 4:17-22; 2 Corinthians 1:3; 10:3; Galatians 5:16; Colossians 3:16; Hebrews 11:1,6,11,12,17-19; James 2:17; Revelation 4:8

Note: Additional options and worksheets in $8^1/_2$" x 11" format for this session are available for download at **www.gospellight.com/uncommon/jh_the_old_testament.zip**.

STARTER

Option 1: Faith Ride. For this option, you will need blindfolds for half of the students, prizes and several obstacles to create an obstacle course. Ahead of time, map out an obstacle course, keeping in mind that the course will be navigated by piggyback, with the carrier blindfolded!

Welcome students and let them know that you're going to start off this session with a game. Pair off students, designating one person in each pair as the "Carrier" and the other as the "Rider." Distribute the blindfolds and instruct the Carriers to wear them, and check to make sure that they can't see. Instruct the Riders to lead the Carriers by the hand to the beginning of the obstacle course, and have them hop on. Riders will verbally guide their Carriers through the course. Warn students that you have the option of moving objects randomly throughout the game to make it more interesting.

The first pair to navigate the course, round-trip, wins the game. Anyone caught peeking will be disqualified! All pairs run the course at the same time. (*Note*: If your group is large or your space is small, you might need to have smaller groups of pairs run the course in heats, and have the winners of each heat run a final heat against one another to determine the winner.)

Award a prize to the winning team, and then read Hebrews 11:1. Explain that faith is trusting and following someone's word, even when we can't see where we're headed. Today we're going to look at a man who is considered to be a model of true faith because he believed God when he couldn't see or understand everything God was telling him.

Option 2: Heart and Mind. For this option, you will need your Bible and a blow dryer (and maybe an extension cord).

Welcome students and read Hebrews 11:1. Explain that to have faith—true faith—is to have true conviction in your heart, rather than just belief in your mind. Now discuss the following:

- What are some things around us that we know exist even though we can't see them? (*Air, radio waves, wind, and so forth.*)
- How do we know they really exist if we can't see them? (*We see their effects and experience them with other senses, such as touch and hearing.*)

Illustrate this last point by turning on the blow dryer and blowing the air on the students. Students can't see the air, but they can feel its effects. Now continue by asking the following:

- How about your brain? Have you ever seen it? (*Hopefully not!*)
- How do you know it exists? (*Because science tells us so—we can't live without one.*)
- How would you define faith? (*Accept several responses, but resist the urge to correct anything yet.*)

Explain that today we're going to look at a man who is considered to be a model of true faith because he believed God when he couldn't see or understand everything God was telling him.

MESSAGE

Option 1: Faith Tic-Tac-Toe. For this option, you will need one copy of "Faith Tic-Tac-Toe" (found on the next page), masking tape, five red baseball caps, five blue baseball caps (or other identifying pieces of cloth or paper), and prizes. Ahead of time, use the masking tape to create a huge Tic-Tac-Toe grid on the floor with squares big enough for someone to stand in.

Begin by stating that we sometimes think of faith as a force or some mystical, unintelligible power. But faith is really a response of trust and obedience to God's Word. One of the best examples of faith in God was Abraham, a man who fully believed God, even when it didn't make sense. God was so pleased with Abraham's response of faith that He blessed Abraham immensely. His example of faith can help our faith grow as well.

Divide students into two teams and distribute the red caps to one team and the blue caps to the other. Explain that each team has just become human *X*s and *O*s for a life-sized game of Tic-Tac-Toe. After you read the Scripture verse(s) listed on the sheet, you will ask one team a question. If they answer it correctly, they can choose a place to send one of their teammates, donning the team color. If they answer it incorrectly, the other team gets a chance to answer and send one of their teammates to a square of their choosing. Next, you'll ask a

Youth Leader Tip

Whenever you are going to be reading aloud, make sure that you practice first! By being prepared, you will convey to your group that what you are reading is not only interesting but also worth hearing.

FAITH
TIC-TAC-TOE

Read Genesis 12:1-5 aloud and ask the following:

- What did God tell Abraham to do? (Leave Haran and set out to a new place.)
- What did God promise to do for Abraham? (Give him a land and use his descendants to bless all families of the earth.)
- How old was he at the time? (75.)
- Where did God tell Abraham to go? (He didn't know where God wanted him to go.)
- Who went with Abraham? (His wife, nephew and "people.")
- What was Abraham's response? (He took God at His word and went.)
- How did Abraham's response show faith in God? (He was willing to set out in obedience, even though he didn't understand the whole plan or have all the answers.)

Read Genesis 15:1-6 and Romans 4:18-22 aloud and ask the following:

- How did God speak to Abraham? (In a vision.)
- What title did Abraham use to address God? (Sovereign Lord.)
- What did Abraham ask of the Lord? (A son.)
- What did God promise to Abraham? (A son and ultimately a family line that would outnumber the stars.)
- How old was Abraham when God gave him this promise? (Almost 100.)
- Did Abraham's faith grow weak when he thought about his age? (No, he considered his age, but he didn't stop believing God.)
- What was Abraham's response to God's promise of a son? (He believed God and took Him at His word. This promise was fulfilled exactly as God said [see Genesis 21:1-3].)

Read Genesis 22:1-18 aloud and ask the following:

- What did God tell Abraham to do? (Offer Isaac as a sacrifice.)
- Did Isaac die? (No, an angel stopped the sacrifice.)
- What was sacrificed? (God sent a ram.)
- How did Abraham's response show faith in God? (He did what God said.)

second question of the other team, and so on. The first team to get three in a row wins that round. There are enough questions to play two rounds, so keep things moving quickly. Explain that you will read a section from the Bible about Abraham, and then they will answer the questions based on what was read. Begin the game, using the handout as your guide.

Award prizes to everyone (yep, the losers, too!) and conclude by reading Numbers 23:19. Explain that faith is not a formula or a force; it's a confident trust that flows from hope in God. Abraham took the time to know God, and so he was filled with hope; and faith was the result. We can cultivate a deeper friendship with God by reading His Word consistently and praying to Him daily. Faith is grounded in who God is, His nature and character. God never lies. His character of truth and perfection means that His Word can be trusted.

Option 2: Immediate Response. For this option, you will need two adult volunteers, two sheets, rope, two secure posts to hang the rope from, a bag of confetti, some sort of prize, a camera with a flash (a digital camera with a laptop computer nearby would be best) and several human obstacles (adults you've instructed to interfere with the volunteer's progress by trying to hold his or her legs or arms).

Ahead of time, create a curtain by tying the rope to two secure posts and hanging the sheets so that there is a way to pass through them but not see what's behind. Have the adult volunteers stand behind the curtains with the confetti before you begin.

Explain that faith begins with a revelation from God. Ever since creation, God has been revealing Himself to humankind so that we could enjoy a close relationship with Him. His love causes us to know Him by opening our minds and hearts to His truth. When He speaks to us about His plan or shows us something about His nature or ways, our part is to respond to Him. That's what faith is: responding in trust and obedience to God, believing and obeying Him. Let's look at three times when Abraham's faith really pleased God. As we think about Abraham's faith, we'll notice several characteristics that we can also make a part of our response to God.

The first time when Abraham's faith pleased God was *when he was called to leave his home.* Ask a volunteer to read Genesis 12:1-5, and then explain that the first two characteristics of faith we see in Abraham's life were that he was fully persuaded and took actions to obey. That meant Abraham totally believed and then did what God revealed to him. It wasn't a well-I-hope-so, we'll-see-how-it-works-out faith, it was a full-on, totally committed trust in God's word;

no questions, no qualifying, just obedience. God told Abraham to leave his hometown of Haran and set out to a new place that God would show him as he went.[1] Abraham took God at His word and left. Abraham didn't know where God wanted him to go, only that he was to pack up his family and leave.

Have a volunteer come to the front. Continue by stating that this would be like you telling this brave volunteer to run through this curtain without knowing what is behind it. He or she doesn't know what's on the other side—it could be a cement wall, a barking dog, a 1,000-foot drop or a bucket of cold water. Hype it up here, getting the anticipation of all the possibilities roused in the group, and then ask the volunteer to run through the curtains. Have him or her start a good distance away to heighten the suspense. When the volunteer passes through the curtains, have one of the adults behind the curtain cheer and take a flash picture and the other adult throw the confetti on him or her. Once he or she has calmed down, award the prize and have the volunteer return to his or her seat.

Explain that responding to your instructions took faith on the part of the volunteer. And, in a much more radical response of faith, Abraham responded to God's instructions and followed His guidance. Thousands of years later, the apostle Paul wrote about Abraham as an example of faith for us. Read Romans 4:20-21 and transition to a personal level by stating that true faith is being *fully* persuaded. When God speaks to us—through His Word or by His Spirit—we need to believe Him and do what He says. Not part way, just dipping our toes in the water, but all the way, jumping in full bore, no holding back.

Continue by stating that true faith is also followed by corresponding actions. Read James 2:17 and explain that it is not enough to just believe; we must put some actions to our faith, like Abraham did. Abraham didn't wait for a map to float down. He didn't say, "Wow! Thanks for thinking of me, God," and then sit in his tent eating cheese puffs. He got up, packed and left, believing that God would show him as he went where he was supposed to go. Faith always shows that it is real by what it does.

The second time when Abraham's faith pleased God was *when he was promised a son.* Tell the group that you will now be jumping forward to another important time in Abraham's life. Abraham is out of his homeland and has increased and prospered beyond his wildest dreams. He is a rich, generous man who is respected and liked by all those around him, but there is one thing he doesn't have—a son, an heir to carry on the family heritage.

Ask a volunteer to read Genesis 15:1-6. Explain that another characteristic of faith that we see in Abraham's life is that he believed God's word in spite of the obstacles—and there were some huge obstacles to this promise happening. When God gave Abraham the promise of a son, he was almost 100 years old and his wife, Sarah, was about 90. A son at their age? That seems like a mistake! God couldn't mean what He said. It's impossible. But true faith doesn't consider anything impossible if it is God's will.

Place several of the human obstacles in front of the curtain and ask for either the same volunteer or a different one to come back and try to make it to the curtain. Undoubtedly, it will be tougher. Explain that these obstacles might have made our volunteer even more timid and afraid of running through the curtain, but Abraham didn't let anything stop him from moving forward. Why? Well, like we've been talking about: he was a man of tremendous faith.

Read Romans 4:17-20, and explain that Abraham didn't deny the obstacles that seemed to make God's promise impossible. He looked at all the reasons why it wouldn't work out, but he didn't let it stop his faith in God. And for us, when God speaks to our hearts about something that seems impossible, we can consider the obstacles but should not let them stop us from believing God. Reread Romans 4:18 aloud, and continue by stating that Abraham believed God—in spite of his age—and God did bless him with a son. It took many years for this promise to happen and Abraham got into a lot of trouble along the way, trying to make the promise happen on his own. But God is so merciful. He kept His word to Abraham, and the promised son, Isaac, was born.

The third time when Abraham's faith pleased God was *when he was asked to sacrifice his son*. Tell the group that you will now fast-forward to another powerful time of faith in the life of Abraham. Have a volunteer read Genesis 22:1-2, and ask the group what God told Abraham to do. (*Offer Isaac up as a sacrifice to Him.*) Continue by asking the group what God was thinking. What would they do if they were Abraham? Allow a few responses, and then ask what response Abraham could have given that would have showed his faith in God. (*To do what God said.*) Next, tell the group that you are going to read about what Abraham did do in this situation.

Youth Leader Tip

When having students find verses in the Bible, always try to pair experienced students with those who are relatively new so that those with experience can explain how to find books, chapters and verses.

Have a volunteer read Genesis 22:3-5 and explain that we started this lesson by explaining that faith is a response of obedience to God. If Abraham's response seems more like stupidity than faith, we need to consider Hebrews 11:17-19. Have a volunteer read the passage , and then explain that Abraham didn't struggle to keep believing God—even in the face of such a painful command—because he had such strong hope in God. That hope came because Abraham had a close relationship with God and an understanding of His nature. He figured that if God asked him to sacrifice Isaac, after it was over God would somehow make a way for him to have another son—perhaps even bring Isaac back from the dead. Abraham believed the promise over the circumstances.

Make this personal by reading aloud Numbers 23:19. Explain that faith is not a formula and it's not a force but a confident trust that flows from hope in God. Abraham took the time to know God and so was filled with hope and faith as a result. We can cultivate a deeper friendship with God by reading His Word consistently and praying to Him daily. Faith is grounded in who God is—His nature and character. God never lies. His character of truth and perfection means that His Word can be trusted. And that is the basis of true faith.

DIG

Option 1: Step of Faith. For this option, you will need several Bibles, the movie *Indiana Jones and the Last Crusade,* and a way to show it to the group. Ahead of time, cue the film to the scene where Harrison Ford's character, Indiana Jones, has to walk across the canyon without being able to see the bridge until he takes the first step.

Show the movie clip, and then discuss the following questions:

- Was there ever a time when you had to take a step of faith? (*Have the group briefly describe it.*)
- How did taking the step help you to grow in your faith? (*Allow for responses.*)
- Why does faith please God? (*Faith shows that we are willing to honor God and His Word above everything else; it is evidence of and impetus for a life of trust and obedience.*)

Explain that faith is not just a force or a mental power; it is a decision to trust God's Word. Our faith in God grows when we know His character—who He is and what He is like. Distribute Bibles and ask volunteers to read the following verses:

- Exodus 15:26 ("the LORD, who heals you")
- Nehemiah 9:31 ("a gracious and merciful God")
- Psalm 145:18-19 ("the LORD is near . . . hears . . . and saves")
- Jeremiah 32:17 ("Sovereign LORD . . . made the heavens and the earth")
- John 11:25 ("the resurrection and the life")
- Acts 4:12 ("Salvation is found in no one else")
- 2 Corinthians 1:3 ("God and Father of our Lord Jesus Christ")
- Revelation 4:8 ("Holy is the Lord God Almighty")

After each verse, stop and discuss how that particular aspect of God's nature could give hope and strengthen faith.

Option 2: The Gift of Faith. For this option, you will need your Bible! Begin by explaining that sometimes faith requires letting go and letting God. Share the following case study:

One evening when Jessica and her 10-year-old brother, David, were walking home after Bible study and youth group, they were approached by a ragged-looking woman.

"Excuse me," the woman said. "I haven't had anything to eat today and I'm hungry. Do you have any money to spare?"

Jessica stood with her hand in her coat pocket, holding the $10 she had saved from baby-sitting, and wondered what she should do. *I know Jesus said to help the poor and the needy, but what if I give her my money and she just uses it to buy drugs or alcohol?* she thought. *I don't want to help this poor woman hurt herself.*

Without hesitation David reached into his coat and took out the entire contents of his pockets: a candy bar, two dimes and a handout from Bible study. "Here," he said to the woman, "you can have this."

The woman looked at David and smiled as she reached out to take what he offered. "What's this, young man?"

"Well," answered David, "tonight at church, we learned about how Jesus is where we should look for help when we're feeling alone or scared. I wrote down reasons why I think I can count on Jesus to be there when I need someone!"

Jessica was very proud of David's willingness to share Jesus and realized that there were other ways to help this woman besides giving her cash. "There's a food pantry at our church," she said. "It's right around the corner and I'm sure they'll give you some food." Then she reached into her pocket and pulled out her favorite Bible. She quickly thumbed through it, glancing at all the marks in it where she had underlined and highlighted verses that had touched her heart. She handed it to the woman, "You can have this too. I've found comfort in it and I'm sure you will too."

The woman took the Bible and thanked David and Jessica for their kindness.

Now discuss the following:

- Was Jessica wrong to hesitate to give the woman money? (*No, because her hesitation actually made it possible for her and David to help the woman even more than what she asked for.*)
- What do you think the woman intended to do with the money? (*There's no way to know for sure.*)
- What if the woman was telling the truth and really would have used the money for food? (*Consider this: If Jessica had given the woman the $10, that might have solved the immediate problem of hunger, but by giving the woman the handout and the Bible, David and Jessica gave her something that will last far longer—the seeds for her spiritual salvation. Also, Jessica's telling her about the food pantry gave the woman the opportunity to find help for herself.*)
- What else could Jessica and David have done to help the woman? (*Well, they could have offered to pray with her and, even if she said no to that, they could have prayed for her.*)
- Okay, so what if there's no food pantry at your church and you don't have a Bible or candy bar in your pocket—what can you do? (*Let students brainstorm here.*)

Continue by stating that there is a saying that goes something like this: "Weave in faith and let God provide the thread." God is forever faithful. When we choose to follow His Word, He will always keep it.

APPLY

Option 1: Do You Believe? For this option, you will need several Bibles, the song "Lord, I Believe in You" sung by Crystal Lewis, and a way to play it. (*Note:*

You can download the song off iTunes or other source or find it on the CD *Gold by Metro One*.)

Read Hebrews 11:6, and then explain that this verse says that to come to God, we must do two things:

1. *Believe that He exists.* Tell the group that this is the first step, and the first question for them to consider is: "Do you believe God exists?" Lead a quiet time of reflection, giving students a chance to search their hearts and see if they have that first connection to faith—belief in a sovereign, personal God who has called them into a special relationship. Emphasize that it is not religion, but honest faith, that connects us to God.

2. *Believe that He rewards those who seek Him.* Explain that this does not mean that a treasure chest of rubies will fall out of the sky, but it does mean that if we seek Him honestly, He will reveal Himself to us. The reward of honest faith is a revelation of who He is. This leads to the second question for the group members to consider: "If you believe that God exists, have you shown your faith by coming to God for forgiveness and salvation?" If not, ask if they are willing to come now.

Play the song "Lord, I Believe in You" and invite students who have not yet accepted Jesus as their personal Savior to take the opportunity right now to ask Him into their hearts. This could be the beginning of faith for them!

Option 2: Are You Contagious? For this option, you will need blank paper, colored felt-tip pens and miscellaneous craft supplies such as stickers and glitter.

Explain that true faith is contagious because people want to believe that God exists, that He relates to them personally and wants to make their life everything it was created to be. God wants us to be a part of sharing that message to those around us.

Use the art supplies to have students design a "No Doubt He Loves You" card, incorporating some of the verses or points from the session (for example, all or part of Psalm 145; Proverbs 3:5-6; 2 Corinthians 10:3; Hebrews 11:6). When the group has finished, have them choose one person to give the card to who needs a faith boost this week. Close the session in prayer, thanking God and asking Him to continue to strengthen them in the knowledge of who He is.

REFLECT

The following short devotions are for the students to reflect on and answer during the week. You can make a copy of these pages and distribute to your class or download and print from **www.gospellight.com/uncommon/jh_ the_old_testament.zip.**

1—THE BEST GIFT EVER

See what God says about faith in Romans 3:22-24 and 6:23.

What is the best gift you have ever received? Whatever that gift is, you probably received it on your birthday or on a holiday, right? But imagine how great it would be if someone were to give you a really cool gift—such as a huge gift certificate to your favorite store or one of those big trampolines for your yard—when it wasn't even your birthday or Christmas or any other holiday! I mean, we expect gifts on our birthdays and holidays, but imagine that this incredible gift was given to you for no reason at all.

In a similar way, God has freely given us an incredible gift: forgiveness for our sins, grace and the chance to have an awesome relationship with Him, all wrapped up in the person of His Son, Jesus Christ. You may be familiar with the verse John 3:16, which says, "For God so loved the world that he gave his one and only Son, that whoever believes in him shall not perish but have eternal life." This gift God gave us cannot be bought or earned; we can only receive God's gift by having faith in Him.

What do you think it means to have faith in God?

_____

_____

_____

Write down a definition for "faith" in the space below, and then share it with someone you think knows a good definition for "faith."

_____

_____

_____

Today, spend some time thinking about this incredible gift that God has given to you free of charge.

2—"FAITHING"

Read what James has to say about faith and works in James 2:14-17.

In English, words that describe actions often end in -ing, such as walking, sitting, playing. In the same way, faith is an action word—even though we wouldn't say "faithing" in English. James's statement that "faith by itself, if it is not accompanied by action, is dead" means that we show that we have faith by what we do or don't do. Basically, we show that we have faith by the way we live.

Can you think of two other action words that have similar meanings to the word "faith"?

_____

_____

_____

On a scale of 1 to 10, how are you doing in showing your faith by your actions? How do you feel about your answer? What would you like it to be?

_____

_____

_____

Today, ask God to help you continually get better at showing your faith in your deeds.

3—BRAVE FAITH

Read Daniel 3:13-28 to hear the story of three friends who went through an amazing ordeal.

Have you ever done something crazy just for the fun of it—like maybe taking a blender dare (drinking a cup of food left over from everyone's meals at a restaurant)? Have you ever done something that seemed really crazy but had a good reason behind it? Well, in this story in Daniel, the three friends had faith, and because of this faith, they did something very risky.

A long time ago, three young friends named Shadrach (Shad-rack), Meshach (Mee-shack) and Abednego (A-bed-nee-go) were kidnapped, along with thousands of their own people, and carried away into a foreign land by a king called Nebuchadnezzar (we will just call him King Neb). Old King Neb really liked himself a lot and decided to make a law stating that all the people in the land should bow down and worship him. He even made a huge statue of himself out of gold for people to worship. But in the land where Shadrach, Meshach and Abednego came from, they only worshiped the one true God. So they would not bow down to King Neb's statue. King Neb became so angry that he ordered the three friends to be thrown into a fiery furnace because they would not bow down to the golden statue.

Think about how the story would have ended if Shadrach, Meshach and Abednego had decided to bow down to the statue when King Neb first threatened them. Ask God to help you have more faith today so that you can be brave like these three men.

4—TENDING THE GARDEN

Read John 15:9-10 to learn one important way to maintain a good relationship with God.

Having relationships with people is hard! Just making friends is hard enough by itself, but keeping friends is a whole other story. It's kind of like keeping a garden. If you don't spend time in the garden pulling weeds and watering plants, after a while you won't have much of a garden left. In the same way, God gives us the gift of having an awesome relationship with Him through our faith in Jesus Christ. (Remember, it's a free gift and it can't be earned!) This relationship needs to be kept up just like a garden. But how do you do that?

What was Jesus' important advice on this in John 15:9-10?

_____

_____

_____

Jesus continues to explain His important advice in verses 12 to 14 of the same chapter. Read John 15:12-14, and then write down the "command."

_____

_____

_____

Think about how you can follow Jesus' advice this week.

JOSEPH: THE BEGINNING OF DELIVERANCE

THE BIG IDEA

Joseph was a deliverer of God's people, but Jesus is our Deliverer who came to save us from our sin.

SESSION AIMS

In this session you will guide students to (1) understand that they need to be delivered from the power of sin; (2) feel the great love of Jesus Christ as their Deliverer; and (3) respond with surrendered hearts to His great grace.

THE BIGGEST VERSE

"You intended to harm me, but God intended it for good to accomplish what is now being done, the saving of many lives. So then, don't be afraid. I will provide for you and your children" (Genesis 50:20-21).

OTHER IMPORTANT VERSES

Genesis 15:13-16; 37–50; Isaiah 59:2; Matthew 7:24-27; Mark 10:45; John 1:10-11,14; 16:33; Acts 7:9-14; 2 Corinthians 4:4; Ephesians 1:17-18; Philippians 2:6-8; Colossians 1:13-14; Hebrews 2:14,17

Note: Additional options and worksheets in 8^1/$_2$" x 11" format for this session are available for download at **www.gospellight.com/uncommon/jh_the_old_testament.zip**.

STARTER

Option 1: Rescue Bingo. For this option, you need copies of "Rescue Bingo" (found on the next page) and pens or pencils.

Greet students and remind them of all the beginnings you've talked about in this series: the beginning of creation, family, sin, worship and faith. Explain that today we'll be looking at the beginning of deliverance. God had a plan to rescue His people from sin, and we see it begin to unfold in the story of Joseph.

Distribute "Rescue Bingo" and pens or pencils. At your signal, students are to walk around and ask someone else in the room if he or she has done any of the things mentioned in the squares. If so, that person signs his or her name on the square. The goal is to be the first person to have an entire row (in any direction) signed. To keep things moving, no one can sign more than two times per paper. When a student completes a row, he should shout "Bingo!"

After someone has won, read the winning row of squares, asking each person who signed to explain briefly about his or her experience. Award the winning player a round of applause, and then transition to the next step by explaining that rescues can be really exciting and rewarding, but they always cost the rescuer something. Rescuing is risky business! The Bible talks about all kinds of rescues, and we're going to look at two of them today.

Option 2: Behind the Fence. For this option, you will need a sturdy rope (at least 20 feet long), two poles, trees or other stationary objects, a notepad and a pen or pencil for keeping score. Ahead of time, tie the rope approximately four feet from the ground between the two poles.

Welcome students and have everyone gather at the rope. Divide the group into teams of 6 to 10 students each and explain that each team is trapped behind an electric fence (the rope). Teams will start out with 100 points each, and the team that successfully rescues its members from behind the fence, with the least amount of points lost, wins!

That's too easy, isn't it? Okay, so each team member must go *over* the fence in order to be rescued. Anyone caught going under or around the fence will be disqualified and his or her team will lose five points. Team members who touch the fence while going over will be "electrocuted," and their team will lose three points. Begin the game by selecting a team to break free first, and when that team has completed its rescue, continue with the next team until all the teams have been freed.

When everyone is done, calculate the points lost by each team and announce the winners. Explain that rescuing is risky business. It costs something

 **RESCUE BINGO**

I've rescued a cat.	I've seen a fire rescue.	I personally know a rescuer.	I've seen a water rescue.	I've heard a siren.
I know the Heimlich maneuver.	I've rescued a friend.	I've seen an air rescue.	I've called 9-1-1 in an emergency.	I've been in the way of a fire truck.
I've petted a trained rescue dog.	I know CPR.	**FREE SPACE**	I've rescued a bird.	I've choked on a test.
I've been rescued.	I've watched a rescue show on TV.	I've rescued a lonely chocolate bar.	I know the helmet maneuver.	I've seen a professional rescue effort.
I've choked on a hot dog.	I can imitate a siren.	I've been in a fire truck.	I know DVD.	I've rescued a family member.

to deliver people, as you found out when you rescued your teammates in the game we just played. This is our last session about beginnings. So far, we have read from Genesis about the beginning of creation, the beginning of family with Adam and Eve, the beginning of sin, the beginning of worship with Noah and the beginning of faith with Abraham. This week we will wrap up everything by looking at what God has to say about the beginning of deliverance. God had a plan to rescue His people from sin, and He began to reveal how it would happen through the life of a slave-turned-ruler named Joseph.

MESSAGE

Option 1: Cue Cards. For this option, you will need your Bible, three sheets of poster board, a felt-tip pen and an inflatable pop-up clown. Ahead of time, use the poster board to create cue cards that read "That's good!" "That's bad!" and "You can't keep a good man down!"

Begin by stating that every rescue requires some sacrifice. We can see some similarities between the sacrifices that Joseph made to deliver his people and the sacrifices that Jesus made to rescue us. Today you are going to look at three main areas of sacrifice, but you will need the group's help. Divide the group into three sections and assign each one a cue-card response. Choose a volunteer from each group to come forward and hold the cue card in front of their group.

Explain that as you tell the group this amazing true story, their job will be to decide if their group has the correct cue-card response to the situation. If it does, they should stand up and shout the response on your cue card. (There might be times when more than one group stands up, in which case you will have to figure out if one sign is more appropriate, or better, than the other.) Be sure to pause after each statement to allow for responses. Now begin to read the statements, noticing the appropriate response to each:

- Joseph came from a large family (11 brothers and 1 sister!), and he was his dad's favorite son. (*That's good!*)[1]
- His dad even had a special coat made for him. (*That's good!*)
- Unfortunately, his jealous brothers hated him. (*That's bad!*)
- Joseph's brothers were going to kill him, but instead they decided to sell him to some traveling merchants, who then took him to Egypt as a slave. (*That's bad!*)
- It would be at least 13 years before he would see his family again. (*That's bad!*)

- But being torn away from his family was actually a part of God's plan. (*You can't keep a good man down!* Hit the inflatable pop-up clown as a visual expression of this statement.)
- Joseph made the best of his new life and served Potiphar, his new owner, well. (*That's good!*)
- He served so well that he was put in charge of the entire household. (*That's good!*)
- Everything Joseph did was blessed and prospered. (*That's good!*)
- But after serving faithfully many years, Joseph was falsely accused by his owner's wife and sent to prison. (*That's bad!*)
- He remained in prison for many years for a crime he didn't commit. (*That's bad!*)
- Even in prison, Joseph continued to trust in God, and God blessed him. (*That's good!*)
- In fact, the warden put Joseph in charge of the whole place. (*You can't keep a good man down!* Hit the inflatable pop-up clown again.)
- Joseph was eventually released from prison and given a place of authority as a ruler in Egypt. (*That's good!*)
- He was given an Egyptian name, wore Egyptian clothes and spoke the Egyptian language. This position of authority was God's plan so that Joseph could have the power to deliver people from a seven-year famine. (*That's good!*)
- The famine came and was so bad that even the neighboring countries were affected. (*That's good!* The students should object to this, but assure them that this is the correct answer.)
- Joseph's brothers came to Egypt for food. Joseph was able to save his family from starvation and help them realize that even though they had meant to harm him, God used the situation to provide deliverance for thousands of people who would have otherwise died from starvation. (*You can't keep a good man down!* You know what to do!)

Youth Leader Tip

Have a competition to see who can come up with the most memorable rap, song or hand motions to go with "The Biggest Verse" for each session. This is a great way to help students hide God's Word in their hearts.

Read Genesis 50:20, and explain that all of the things that happened to Joseph were a part of God's plan of deliverance. Joseph's sacrifices allowed God to use him to rescue a lot of people. Jesus, too, sacrificed His identity in order to rescue us. Philippians 2:6-8 tells us that He put on human flesh and became one of us so that He could deliver us from the death caused by sin. The ultimate sacrifice of His life provided a way for us to be cleansed from sin and restored to a right relationship with God.

Continue by stating that like Joseph, Jesus was also torn away from His home. He wasn't forced to leave, however, as Joseph was. Jesus left by choice, to do the will of His Father. Jesus served His Father faithfully. He lived a perfect life of obedience and integrity. Yet, like Joseph, He was falsely accused, misunderstood and eventually killed. Even though Jesus could have come as a powerful king, He came as a humble servant and hung out with the outcasts of society. He sacrificed His reputation to reach the lost people His Father loved.

Sum up by stating that Jesus sacrificed His home, His reputation and His identity to deliver us because He loves us. Read Colossians 1:13-14, and conclude by stating that the sacrifices Jesus made were for us! That's good!

Option 2: From Pits to Palaces. For this option, you will need to carefully study this lesson, because it's got a lot of information in it!

Begin by stating that when we first began this series on Genesis, we learned that God specifically and carefully designed this world and everything in it, including people like you and me. In fact, mankind—both male and female—was the crowning work of His creation. Unfortunately, that perfect place and close relationship that God designed us to experience was forever marred when Adam and Eve chose to eat that piece of forbidden fruit. By their disobeying God's Word, sin captured their hearts and locked them and all their descendants out of intimate fellowship with God.

Continue by stating that the story could have stopped there, but it didn't. Because of how much God loves His people, He had a plan to rescue them. At the right time He would send a Deliverer to free us from the power of sin and reopen that door to relationship with Him. Our understanding of God's plan for deliverance begins with the life of Joseph. He was a deliverer for God's people at that time, pointing us to the day when *the* Deliverer, Jesus Christ, would come to rescue us.

State that we need to get up to speed from our last session. God promised Abraham to make him a father of many nations. At that time, Abraham didn't even have a child of his own, but Abraham believed God's promise and ended up with a son, Isaac. Isaac had two sons, the twins Jacob and Esau. Jacob went on to have 12 sons, who became known as the 12 tribes of Israel, and later just Israel. All Jewish people derive their heritage from these 12 sons—even those who live in the country of Israel today. Joseph was one of Jacob's sons—his favorite son, to be exact, which didn't make family relations very happy. But God used the awful things that happened to Joseph to ultimately deliver His people.

Read Genesis 37:2-28. Explain that Joseph's life started with a good dream and ended with a bad deal. Joseph's dream was from God, and it showed him something that would happen in the future. Joseph would need to hang on to that dream in the same way that Abraham hung on to God's promise of a son, because there would be years of hard times ahead of him. Unwisely, Joseph shared his dream with his already jealous brothers, and they decided it was time to get rid of him. They sold him to traveling merchants who resold him to an Egyptian official named Potiphar. That could have been the end of Joseph's dreams, but it wasn't. That unfortunate turn of events actually was part of God's plan of deliverance. He wanted Joseph to be in Egypt, and that's where he was taken.

Now read Genesis 39:1-23. Explain that rather than moping about his situation, Joseph determined to do the best he could for his new owner. God honored Joseph's commitment and blessed his work so much that Potiphar put him in charge of his whole household. Things were going great until Potiphar's wife put the moves on Joseph and she was humiliated when he refused to have anything to do with her. To get even, she falsely accused him, and Potiphar put Joseph in another pit—the king's prison. This too could have seemed like the end of Joseph's dream, but it wasn't. In prison Joseph met someone who would connect him to Pharaoh, which was another part of God's plan of deliverance.

Next, read Genesis 41:1-40. Explain that after two long years, Joseph was taken out of prison and was made Pharaoh's right-hand man. In one day, God brought him from being a forgotten prisoner to a celebrated second-only-to-the-king official. This too was part of God's plan. God wanted Joseph to have authority to make big decisions and put him in a place where he could—and would—do just that. Joseph's decisions saved multitudes of people from a devastating seven-year famine.

Read Genesis 42:1-6 and explain that the famine had gotten so bad that even the surrounding lands were affected. Because of Joseph's careful planning, Egypt was the only place to get grain. So Jacob sent his 10 oldest sons there for food. When the brothers came, they bowed down, not knowing it was Joseph they were bowing down before. Sound familiar? Joseph's dream had come true.

It had been 13 years since they sold him into slavery; and they never expected to see him again—let alone as Pharaoh's second in command. They didn't even recognize Joseph. But Joseph recognized his brothers and later revealed his identity to them.

Read Genesis 45:4-8 and explain that Joseph had them go back to get Jacob and move to Egypt so that their families would have enough food to last the famine. He pulled a few royal strings and arranged for good land and jobs. His jealous, hateful brothers were afraid that Joseph would take revenge on them, but instead Joseph saw the whole thing as the sovereign plan of God to provide deliverance for His people.

Conclude by reading Genesis 50:20. Explain that for Joseph, the pit led to slavery in Egypt, which led to him being bought by Potiphar, which led to him being thrown in prison, which led to him interpreting dreams for Pharaoh, which led to him obtaining a position of authority, which led to his wise planning, which led to thousands of people receiving food during a long famine, which ultimately led to deliverance for his own family.

Tell the group that this story relates to the deliverance that Jesus provides for us. Joseph was *a* deliverer, but Jesus is *the* Deliverer, whose sacrifice made it possible for us to experience freedom from the power of sin. He left His home in heaven, became like us and offered up His own life to deliver us. Read Colossians 1:13-14 and state that Jesus sacrificed His home, reputation, identity *and* His own life to deliver us because He loves us—you and me!

DIG

Option 1: Joseph's Story/Jesus' Story. For this option, you will need several Bibles, copies of "Joseph's Story/Jesus' Story" (found on the next page) and pens or pencils.

Ask the group if anyone can tell you some of the beginnings that you've talked about during this unit. (*Creation, family, sin, worship and faith.*) Continue

Youth Leader Tip
Know your strengths and weaknesses as a leader. Allow student and adult volunteers to use their abilities to come alongside you where you need help. This will not only help you, but it will equip them to serve as well.

Joseph's Story / Jesus' Story

Read your group's assigned passages and compare how Joseph's and Jesus' stories were similar.

Your group's assigned passages are: _____

Questions	Joseph's Story	Jesus' Story
Who were the main people involved?		
What happened?		
What was the main person's response?		
What personal sacrifices were made?		
What happened to others as a result?		

Common Denominator

Now read Genesis 50:20 and discuss how this verse applies to both Joseph and Jesus.

by stating that just as sin had a beginning, so did salvation—God had a plan to rescue us from the power of sin. Today, the group is going to take a look at the beginning of God's plan for deliverance by comparing the life of Joseph as a deliverer for his people and Jesus as the ultimate Deliverer of God's people.

Read Acts 7:9-14 and explain that this passage summarizes the story of Joseph's life from Genesis 37–50. Ask the group to note that there are some interesting similarities between the lives of Joseph and Jesus.[2] Distribute "Joseph's Story/Jesus' Story" and pens or pencils, and then divide students into three groups. Assign each group one of the following passages:

Group 1:   Genesis 37 and John 1:10-11
Group 2:   Genesis 39 and Philippians 2:6-8
Group 3:   Genesis 41, John 1:14 and Hebrews 2:14,17

Have each group complete their assigned portion of the handout. When they have all finished, regroup and allow each of the groups to share their passages and answers. As students are sharing, make sure that the following information surfaces:

- In Genesis 37, Joseph was rejected by his jealous brothers and sold into slavery. Jesus was also rejected by His "brothers," the Jews (see John 1:10-11). Both Joseph and Jesus gave up their families or homes as part of God's plan for deliverance.

- In Genesis 39, Joseph was unjustly thrown into prison. Jesus was also falsely accused and suffered the loss of His reputation in order to reach the outcasts and lost people of the world (see Philippians 2:6-8).

- In Genesis 41, Joseph was made a ruler in Egypt and through the wisdom of God was able to avoid certain starvation for Egypt as well as surrounding peoples. This deliverance required him to sacrifice his birth identity and talk, dress and live as an Egyptian. Jesus, too, sacrificed His identity when He came as a flesh-and-blood human being. Though He never ceased to be God, He did clothe Himself in humanity, identifying with us, so that He could ultimately save us (see John 1:14; Hebrews 2:14,17).

After the students have shared, discuss the following questions:

- In each passage that you read, some major sacrifices were made in order for God's plan of deliverance to happen. Were the sacrifices all by choice? (*For Joseph, his sacrifices were not made by choice, but he did choose to trust that God would bring about justice—and He did. Jesus chose to sacrifice out of His love for us.*)

- How did trust in God carry Joseph and Jesus through hard times? (*Knowing the faithfulness of God, they were able to commit the hardship to Him, trusting that He would use it to accomplish His purpose.*)

- Love was their motivation for persevering faith. How can this help us face an unwanted sacrifice? (*When we are put in a place where we must sacrifice, we can trust God that His plan is being worked out through the difficulty and that something of eternal good will result.*)

Option 2: Unknown Dangers. For this option, you will need the facts, and nothin' but the facts! Read the following case study:

Justine spent all of her spare time talking to her friends on the Internet. Although Justine's parents warned her not to go into chat rooms, they didn't know that she could post a profile in a member directory, telling anyone who looked through it some of her personal information. Since Justine's parents didn't tell her she couldn't post her profile, she didn't think there would be anything wrong with filling one out, so like all of her girlfriends from school, she listed boys in the hobby category.

Gradually, Justine made lots of online friends, and her buddy list kept growing. She especially liked one online friend named Erica. Erica's profile said she was the same age as Justine, and they seemed to have a lot in common. The more comfortable Justine became with Erica, the more personal information Justine gave. Before long, Erica and Justine were discussing their favorite stores at the local mall and their favorite after-school activities.

Justine wasn't aware of it, but Erica wasn't a 13-year-old girl. "Erica" was actually a man in his 30s named Eric who was a convicted child molester. Thankfully, though Justine didn't know this, the police did; and they were monitoring Eric's Internet activities, hoping to catch him before he could hurt anyone again. When Justine and "Erica" made arrangements to meet at the mall on Saturday, undercover police officers were there to arrest Eric and protect Justine from harm.

Discuss the following questions:

- Did Justine know she needed rescuing? (*No, she assumed that Erica's profile was as honest as hers was.*)

- How might Justine have felt if someone had told her that Erica might not be who she claimed to be? (*She might have thought that person was overreacting.*)

- Have you ever felt like someone was overreacting in order to protect you from a hidden danger, like when your mom or dad told you that you couldn't walk to the convenience store at 10 P.M.? Explain.

- Have you ever realized later that your parents were right to say no to something you wanted to do? Explain.

State that we don't always know when we need to be rescued, but Jesus knows the dangers we face in our sins, and He sacrificed His home in heaven to come here and rescue us. We can't actually see heaven and hell right now, but we do need Jesus' deliverance to bring us out of a future in hell and into heaven with Him!

APPLY

Option 1: Success Where It Counts. For this option, you will need several Bibles (loaners and gift Bibles), a notepad and a pen.

Begin by asking the group what they want to do with their lives. Listen to several answers, and then ask each student why he or she wants to do that (for money, for prestige, for the satisfaction of helping people, because it is interesting, and so forth). Now ask them what they think defines success in this world. (*Money, power, material possessions.*)

Distribute Bibles and ask a volunteer to read Matthew 7:24-27. Then state the following:

Each day that we are alive, we are given 86,400 seconds. That's 1,440 minutes every single day. We can do a lot of things in that time and make a lot of choices. But no matter what we do with our lives, if we don't build them on a solid foundation, we are absolutely going to fail in the one area that every single person who has ever lived has an equal opportunity for success: eternal life with our Father in heaven. You can become anything on this earth [name some of the students' answers to what they want to be] and you can be a success here, but by accepting the deliverance that Jesus Christ offers, you become successful in the most important area of your whole existence: a meaningful relationship with God.

Invite students who haven't received Jesus as their personal Savior but would like to make that commitment now to see you at the end of the session— and invite anyone to stay who would like to support their friends as they begin a new life in Christ. After the session, pray with those who would like to receive the gift of salvation and present them with a gift Bible, writing their names and the date on the inside. Record their names and phone numbers so that you can call each one and encourage him or her in the upcoming week.

End the session with a prayer of thanksgiving to Jesus Christ for His awesome gift of deliverance from our sins, and ask Him to encourage students in the coming week to look to Him for guidance in all of their decisions.

Option 2: Be a Life Saver. For this option, you will need several Bibles, index cards, LifeSaver® candies and pens or pencils.

Distribute Bibles, index cards and pens or pencils and invite students to write the names of their unsaved family and friends on the cards. Invite them to form small prayer circles of three to five, and ask each group to read 2 Corinthians 4:4 and Ephesians 1:17-18. As they read the verses, invite the groups to pray for each friend or a family member by name.

Challenge students to pray every day for the people listed on their cards that God would provide opportunities in the coming weeks to plant the seeds for His harvest. Encourage them to keep praying every day and to watch God's awesome power as He provides opportunities for planting.

Close in prayer, thanking God for the grace and mercy that allow us to come to Him on behalf of those we care about and asking Him to help us to bring Him a great harvest of people for His kingdom. Distribute the LifeSaver® candies to students as they leave, as a reminder of their desire to be involved as God rescues others around them.

REFLECT

The following short devotions are for the students to reflect on and answer during the week. You can make a copy of these pages and distribute to your class or download and print from **www.gospellight.com/uncommon/jh_ the_old_testament.zip.**

1—LUCKY OR DELIVERED?

To find out who is our true deliverer, read 2 Samuel 22:1-2.

Daniel couldn't believe how his walk home from school had been. First, he was almost hit by a skateboarder coming down the sidewalk super fast. Then a tile fell off the new drugstore roof and narrowly missed his head. Then a driver didn't see him as he was crossing the street and slammed on his brakes just before hitting him. When Daniel got home, he told his brother, "Wow, I am the luckiest person I know. Good thing I had my lucky socks on today, or I'm sure one of those things would have hurt me."

If you were Daniel's brother, what would you say to him?

_____

_____

_____

God is our ultimate Deliverer. Think back over your week. What are two ways that God has delivered you from harm?

_____

_____

_____

Thank God for the many, many ways that He protects you. And next time something almost happens to you, make sure you thank the right Deliverer.

2—WHICH NEED?

Feeling needy? Check out Psalm 40:17.

Which one of these needs would God be the best at meeting?

- ❏ An infant born with lungs that don't seem to work on their own
- ❏ A lonely eighth-grader who is just sure that all her friends hate her

❑ A family who searches their kitchen to scrounge up enough food to make dinner

❑ A 75-year-old man lying in a hospital bed, who is afraid that he is going to hell

God can meet any need we have, whether it is emotional, physical, financial or spiritual. But that last type of need is the most important. Our biggest need is for spiritual deliverance, which He's provided in sending Jesus to die and be resurrected for us, and now He offers us forgiveness from our sins.

Thank God for one need you've had recently that He has taken care of for you. Actually, why don't you thank Him for two? Or maybe even three? Who knows? Maybe you can come up with as many needs that God has met as the number of years in your age (meaning if you're 12, you come up with 12 needs God has taken care of for you).

3—GOD, OUR FORT

Look up Psalm 18:2 for some ways on how to describe God.

Matt and Kimie just loved building forts in their living room. Pillows, sofas, cushions, sheets, chairs, walls, and even ceilings were all fair game for their enormous homemade forts. Once the forts were built, they would run upstairs to their bedrooms and grab every sock they could find. They would ball them up and hide behind their forts and throw them at each other. Sure, the sheets would collapse and sometimes the cushions would fall down, but Matt and Kimie didn't care. They loved hiding in those forts and throwing socks at each other.

How is God like a fort? Does He ever collapse?

_____

_____

_____

What is something that is bugging you or causing you to worry? How can you find refuge, or safety, in God from this?

_____

_____

_____

Today, ask God to show you how to run to Him whenever you have questions.

4—I'M SCARED!

Feeling scared? Then turn to Psalm 34:4.

Okay, so you are not afraid of the dark any longer and you have packed away that night-light. But are there other things that you are afraid of? For instance, are you afraid that . . .

- ❑ You won't get asked to the big party next weekend?
- ❑ Your mom and dad will get a divorce?
- ❑ The girl or guy you like will think you're a dork?
- ❑ You won't get into a good college?
- ❑ Your grandma will die soon?

If you're honest with yourself, there are probably all sorts of things you're afraid of. What does Psalm 34:4 say about God and your fears?

_____

_____

_____

What is the one thing that is really making you afraid right now?

_____

_____

_____

Do you believe that God can deliver you from that fear? Why or why not?

_____

_____

_____

If you truly believe God can deliver you, then go ahead and ask Him to do so. If you do not, then ask Him to give you more faith so that you can be full of faith—not fear—this week.

GET TO KNOW THE BOOKS OF THE OLD TESTAMENT

These first six sessions have given you an overview of many of the events found in Genesis. In the next section, we will look at some of the "heroes of the faith" from other books in the Old Testament. These were people who heard God's call, acted on their faith, and took incredible risks to do what God told them to do. Before we look at these characters, it might be good to first review the books of the Old Testament to see why scholars have grouped certain ones together.

The Books of the Law

Also known as the *Torah* ("Instruction") or *Pentateuch* ("Five Books"), these consist of the books of Genesis through Deuteronomy. Genesis begins with the creation of the world and ends with the story of Joseph in Egypt. Exodus and Numbers tell the story of the Israelites' bondage in Egypt and their long journey to the Promised Land. Leviticus contains laws and priestly rituals that the people were to follow. Deuteronomy contains three sermons delivered by Moses before the Israelites crossed into the Promised Land in which he reviewed what they been through since leaving Egypt, reminded them of their covenant with God, and challenged them to follow God as they looked to the future.

Historical Books

These consist of the books of Joshua through Esther and tell the history of the nation of Israel. Joshua shows how God enabled the Israelites to capture the Promised Land. Judges depicts some of the men and women that God called to lead the young nation. First Samuel through 2 Chronicles tells the history of Israel after it became a monarchy and how the nation was eventually divided into two separate kingdoms: Israel in the north and Judah in the south. Each of these books also show how the people repeatedly disobeyed God and broke the covenant He had established, ultimately resulting in their exile from the land. Ezra and Nehemiah show how the Lord brought some of the exiles back to the land, while Ruth and Esther contain individual accounts of two women in different circumstances who had incredible faith in God.

Wisdom Books

These consist of the books of Job through Song of Songs and are so named because they teach wisdom about God and godly living. Job tells the story of a man who endured many trials, his discussions with friends about his suffering, his challenge to God, and God's response. Psalms consists of 150 songs and prayers to God, almost half of which are attributed to King David, on a variety of different subjects. Proverbs lists a number of short sayings intended to teach truths about how God wants a person to live. Ecclesiastes, one of the more depressing books in the Bible, contains reflections on the meaninglessness of life without God at the center. Song of Songs, perhaps the most controversial Old Testament book, relates the romantic dialogue between a man and his bride.

Major Prophets

These books, so named because of the length of the work rather than the importance of the authors, consist of the books of Isaiah through Daniel. The prophets' role was primarily to warn God's people that if they did not turn from their ways, they would have to suffer the consequences of their disobedience. Scholars believe that the prophets proclaimed their messages for a little over 300 years, from the time of Jonah in 770 B.C to the time of Malachi in 433 B.C.

Minor Prophets

This final grouping consists of the books of Hosea through Malachi and represents some of the shorter messages the prophets delivered to God's people. (Obadiah, at just 21 verses, is the shortest book in the Old Testament.)

Now that you've got an idea of what you will find in the Old Testament, spend some time reading from each of these books. When you do, you will learn more about not only the people featured in the stories but also about God Himself and how He loves each and every one of us.

UNIT II

Heroes of the Faith

Real life—or even something that just appears to be real life—can grab a junior-higher's attention like almost nothing else can. That is why this series of Bible studies on the heroes of the faith can be such a strategic tool for teaching your students. It gives them a chance to see real-life people facing real-life issues in the hands of a real-life God. These heroes of the Old Testament will give your junior-highers a great chance to see how the real-life Word of God intersects with their real-life worlds.

Kids Want a Hero

Whether it is Kobe Bryant, LeBron James, Lady Gaga or Harry Potter, kids are drawn to personalities from whom they can gain a sense of identity. Exposing your students to the stories of young people like Daniel, who was willing to risk his life to be faithful to his God, or Samuel, who at a young age heard the voice of God, or Esther, who risked everything to save her people, gives your students a chance to meet the kind of heroes that don't get much press in pop culture.

Kids Want to Hear a Story

William Kilpatrick, in his book *Why Johnny Can't Tell Right from Wrong,* argues that one of the reasons moral education has taken such a nosedive in this culture is because we have forgotten the power of good stories told well.

When I was a little boy, my parents always warned me about venturing too far out into the ocean. They told me that there might be a riptide, an undertow or any other number of dangers lurking out there. I knew the ocean as nothing more than a vast, watery playground inhabited by animals like Flipper and Shamu. At least, that was what I thought until I saw the movie *Jaws.* From that day on everything changed! It used to be, "Last one in is a rotten egg!" Now, it was more like, "Mom, why don't you and Dad go in first?" Almost overnight my attitudes about the ocean shifted dramatically. Why? Because I had been given a very vivid account of what could happen in that watery playground— and I didn't want to play anymore.

Such is the power of stories—even though I knew that *Jaws* wasn't a true one! A good story well told can shape us and mold our perceptions in profound ways. No wonder Jesus never began His teaching with the words, "My topic today is on forgiveness." Instead, it was, "There was a man who had two sons." Once upon eternity.

Kids Respond to Realness

Have fun with these studies. Don't try to sanitize the gritty details of the biblical figures who, though virtuous, also had real-life flaws and sins. Don't sacrifice the telling of the story so that you can hammer home the moral. Just let God speak through His Word. These stories that you will be studying have been shaping the faith and history of people since the beginning of time. Enjoy this opportunity to give your junior-highers a taste of the real Word!

Duffy Robbins
Professor of Youth Ministry
Eastern University, St. Davids, Pennsylvania

MOSES: DELIVERING GOD'S PEOPLE

THE BIG IDEA

God delivered Moses and then in turn used him as a deliverer. He wants to do the same in our lives too, making us delivered deliverers.

SESSION AIMS

During this session you will guide students to (1) learn the story of the Exodus; (2) realize that God wants them to experience His delivering power personally; and (3) pinpoint specific ways that He is preparing them to be agents of deliverance to others.

THE BIGGEST VERSE

"So now, go. I am sending you to Pharaoh to bring my people the Israelites out of Egypt" (Exodus 3:10).

OTHER IMPORTANT VERSES

Exodus 1:7-14,22; 2:1-19; 3:1-13,29-31; 5:1-2; 7:14-25; 8:1-30; 9:1-35; 10:1-29; 11:1-10; 12:29-30; Acts 7:22; Hebrews 11:23-28

Note: Additional options and worksheets in 8$^1/_2$" x 11" format for this session are available for download at **www.gospellight.com/uncommon/jh_the_old_testament.zip**.

STARTER

Option 1: Luckiest Person Alive. For this option, you will need a story of your own about a time when you were extremely "lucky." You will also need a laptop computer in order to show a short YouTube clip.

Begin by asking students to share situations when they were really "lucky." Maybe they found themselves in a dangerous situation and were rescued, or perhaps they were given something they did not expect and could never have gotten on their own. Share your own "lucky" story as well. Once the stories are flowing and the students are reveling in their great good fortune, show a short video clip that features a man who should have been killed but wasn't. (You can find these clips on YouTube by searching "luckiest man" or similar phrases.[1] There are many to choose from, but be sure to watch anything you select all the way through and evaluate the entire content of the clip for suitability before you show it.)

After you've watched the clip and everyone has picked up their jaws from the floor, discuss the difference between luck and sovereignty. Help them understand that God can and does powerfully enforce His will, and sometimes that results in what some would call luck. In truth, though, it's His sovereignty being expressed in unexpected events and miraculous intervention. Today's message centers on how God in His sovereignty staged one of the most defining rescue stories in history. (What a lucky day that was!)

Option 2: Reenacted Rescues. For this option, you need a bunch of extroverted students who like to ham it up, a "prop" box full of odds and ends that could be used as makeshift props (for example, rope, cloth, hats, flowers, hula hoops, last week's donuts—basically anything left lying around the church activity room), a timer and a bag full of prizes.

Begin by asking students to get into groups of three to four. Give them five minutes to secretly plan a short skit that reenacts a famous rescue scene from a well-known book or movie. These could be anything from fairy tales to action movies—anything that involves someone being saved from danger. As the groups plan, take the "prop" box around and have each group select one prop *to give to another group*. The assigned prop must be creatively used in their presentation. If the students are stumped for famous rescues, encourage them to think about children's books, Disney movies, war stories, and so forth. There are plenty of rescues to be had!

Have each group take turns presenting their rescue, including a creative use of the assigned prop. After everyone is finished, applaud frenetically and award prizes (you can do mini Oscar speeches if you want . . . best reenactment, best use of prop, best director, and so forth), and then ask students which stories appeal to them most and why. Help students think about why rescues are exciting: the impossible is overcome, the underdogs are freed, the unlikely become heroes, the bad guys get what they deserve, and so on. Hopefully, they will come to see that rescues engender in us a sense of wonder, gratefulness and hope. Let them know that today they'll be learning about one of the most defining rescues in all of human history—one so amazing it even touches our lives thousands of years later. No props required.

MESSAGE

Option 1: Rescued to Rescuer. For this option, you need several Bibles, several copies of "Rescued to Rescuer" (found on the next page), and pens or pencils.

By way of background, explain that the Exodus of Israel from Egypt is the defining story of the Old Testament. It's the time when God moved to free a people who neither deserved nor merited His divine intervention. It was out of His love and providence that He rescued them from cruel bondage and made them His people. The whole Israelite identity is based on this act of liberation, and at the center of God's plan is an unlikely deliverer: Moses.

Distribute Bibles, pens or pencils, and copies of "Rescued to Rescuer." Have students turn to Exodus. Explain that at the end of Genesis, the Hebrew tribes had been invited to move to Egypt because of the great service Joseph provided in saving the country from a seven-year famine (see session 6). The Hebrew tribes had been welcomed by the pharaoh himself and encouraged to settle down and prosper. After many years, the tides of favor turned, and that's where Exodus picks up the history. We learn about the trouble the Israelites stumbled into and how God rescued them using Moses. Moses' story is important in two ways: first, it shows us that God wants to rescue us personally; and second, it teaches us that He wants to use us to help bring His rescue to others.

Have students work in pairs to complete the "Moses the Rescued" side of the handout. They may need your guidance, so be sure to circulate around the room while they are working. Once the students have completed the first side, regroup and talk through their responses. An important theme to highlight is that Moses' rescue was something *initiated and executed by God's sovereignty.* Many babies were being thrown into the Nile, which the Egyptians believed had magical powers, but it was by God's providence that Moses was kept from drowning, escaped the dangers of the river (including aggressive crocodiles,

RESCUED TO RESCUER

Moses the Rescued	Moses the Rescuer
Exodus 1:7-8 What was significant about this new ruler of the Egyptians?	**Exodus 2:11-15** How did Moses try to rescue the Hebrew people?
Exodus 1:9-14 What did Pharaoh order be done to the Hebrews?	**Exodus 2:16-19** How did Moses rescue the shepherd girls?
Exodus 1:22 What did Pharaoh order be done to the baby boys?	**Exodus 3:7-10** Who is going to rescue the Israelites? Whom is He sending as a rescuer?
Exodus 2:1-4 What did Moses' mom do to save him?	**Exodus 4:12-13** What was Moses' response to this rescue idea?
Exodus 2:5-10 How was Moses rescued?	**Exodus 4:29-31** What did Moses do?

poisonous snakes, angry hippopotami and scorpions), was found by a woman who could grant him immunity, and was allowed to be raised by his own mother until he was old enough to be taken into the home of the princess herself. God rescued Moses when he had nothing to offer and nothing to give back. It was simply because of God's great mercy and divine purpose.

Have the group members pair up again to complete "Moses the Rescuer." After the students have had time to respond, gather together and discuss their answers. This time, help them see that Moses, having been rescued himself, turns out to be a rescuer . . . even though he made some mistakes along the way. At first, he tries to rescue the Hebrews in his own strength by killing an oppressive Egyptian, but then he ends up having to flee the country himself. In the desert, he rescues the shepherd girls (see Genesis 2:15-16) and even waters their camels (unheard of work for a man!), but then ends up spending 40 years living in the desert as a shepherd until God Himself initiates the rescue Moses tried to accomplish as a young man. By that time Moses was not the brave hero he once was—God had to *make* him go.

Close by explaining how Moses' own "exodus" (see Exodus 1–5) parallels the exodus of the Israelites in many ways (see Exodus 5–15). Both experience deliverance from Egyptian oppression, both spend 40 years in the desert learning to trust God, and both discover the power of God's sovereign mercy as the ultimate Rescuer. So, as a baby, Moses was rescued by God's divine power and plan, and then, as a man, Moses was used by God's divine power and plan to be a rescuer of others.

Option 2: Tell Me a Story. For this option, you'll need a fire pit with a blazing fire and some mad storytelling skills. (*Note:* If you have your meetings at night and can hold them outside, this is a great option to consider because of the effect a blazing fire has when used as a focal point to the burning bush story.)

Ask students if they've ever heard of the expression "being on the backside of the desert." Solicit responses and then explain (if needed) that it refers to someone who has had to take a long detour away from his goals and is stuck in a lonely, unfruitful place—kind of like being the perennial benchwarmer on a sports team, the one who never gets to actually play the game.

Next, ask them if they've ever heard the expression "a burning bush." Solicit responses and tell them (again, if needed) that it refers to a miraculous event that gives direction or purpose to someone. Explain that both expressions come from the book of Exodus and the story of a guy who experienced a burning bush while on the backside of the desert.[2]

Here's where your mad storytelling skills come in. Explain the major events of Exodus 1–15, the story of Moses and the Exodus. While the students are gazing at the roaring flames in the fire pit, be compelling, be engaging, and be sure you include these points:

- Pharaoh had conscripted the Israelites into forced labor, massively oppressing them.

- Moses was miraculously rescued from death as a baby and grew up as a son of an Egyptian princess.

- Moses tried to rescue the Hebrews on his own and ended up fleeing for his life to a desert called Midian, where he spent 40 years on the backside of the desert.

- God appeared to Moses in a burning bush and told him to go back to Egypt because He was going to use him to rescue the Hebrews.

- God revealed himself to Moses as the great I AM, which forever changed the way all Israel understood the nature of God.

- Moses tried to refuse, but God wouldn't let him. Moses was the one God had chosen to use as a deliverer—and Moses was the one who was going.

- God used Moses to do some amazing miracles, including the famous 10 plagues, and he led His people to freedom.

DIG

Option 1: God vs. gods. You will need several Bibles, copies of "God vs. gods" (found on the following page) and pens or pencils. (*Note*: A leader reference guide is included in the worksheet files that are available online for download.)

Begin by explaining that when Moses went to give Pharaoh God's message, "Let My people go" (Exodus 5:1), it wasn't well received. Pharaoh wasn't about to give up his labor force because some puny tribal god said so . . . or at least that's what he thought at first (see Exodus 5:2). The miracles that God did through Moses amount to nothing less than a showdown between some of the Egyptian gods and the great I AM. These miracles were meant to reveal God's power and to show the world the glory of the one true God.

Give each student a Bible, a copy of "God vs. gods" and a pen or pencil. Have students work in small groups to read about the plagues and complete

GOD vs. gods

Each of these passages deals with one of the 10 plagues. Read the passage and jot down some of the things that happened.

Exodus 7:14-24	Exodus 9:8-12
Exodus 8:1-15	Exodus 9:13-35
Exodus 8:16-19	Exodus 10:1-20
Exodus 8:20-32	Exodus 10:21-29
Exodus 9:1-7	Exodus 11:1-10; 12:29-30

the handout. If it's too much for your students to do the whole activity, divide up the information and have each group look up a few of the plagues and then report back their findings to everyone.

When they have finished, go over the responses using the reference guide available online to fill in any gaps and add details about the specific Egyptian deities. Help students see the way many of the plagues are direct refutations of Egyptian deity and how the rest show God's power over many aspects of the Egyptians' daily lives. Explain that the plagues weren't the result of Moses' magic but of God's power against the oppressors of His people. God used plagues for the specific purpose of exalting His Name and showing the Egyptians that their gods were not supreme. By the last plague, everyone realized there was only one God worthy of worship and obedience: the great I AM!

Option 2: 40-40-40. For this option, you need some masking tape. Ahead of time, mark off three big areas so that you and your students can move from one to the other as you discuss the three major periods of Moses' life. If you want, you can make three giant "40s" in each area with the tape.

Begin by asking the students where they expect to be and what they expect to be doing when they're 40. (Forty seems like a lifetime away to a teen, but assure them that people do indeed live that long and, for the most part, still have the ability to be productive members of society.) Continue by explaining that the life of Moses can be broken into three 40-year periods: (1) the 40 years Moses spent in Egypt as a "somebody," (2) the 40 years he spent in the desert as a "nobody," and (3) the 40 years he spent as a rescuer of Israel. Let's look at each of those years and see what they show us about following God.

- *Moses as a somebody.* Have the whole group move into the first area marked off by masking tape. Explain that the first 40 years were spent in Egypt. Ask them what kind of things they think Moses learned during this time. It was certainly a time of privilege. The Bible teaches us that Moses was schooled in "all the wisdom of the Egyptians" (Acts 7:22). This meant he knew not only the religious system, which would prove useful when God sent him to challenge the pharaoh and his gods, but Moses also learned how to build cities, write books, and manage people—all of which would be useful when he was leader of the Israelites. Unfortunately, Moses was so sure of his abilities that he took it upon himself to initiate their rescue. He honestly thought everyone would recognize that God had called him to be a deliverer, but they didn't. Moses' first 40 years ended with his fleeing to the desert in order to avoid the murder charge he deserved.

- *Moses as a nobody.* Have the whole group move into the second area marked off by masking tape. Explain that the second 40 years were spent in Midian, a desert. Moses seemed to have kind of given up on his idea of being a rescuer. He marries a girl and settles down to be a shepherd. Ask students what they think he learned during his stay in the wilderness. One of the most salient lessons was probably how to survive in the desert—which would prove to be really helpful when he was leading the whole Israelite nation around one!

- *Moses as a rescuer.* Have the whole group move into the third area marked off by the masking tape. Explain that the last 40 years were spent as the leader of a huge nation that had been divinely chosen and sovereignly rescued by the one true God, the great I AM. Moses learned to wait for God's timing, to act in obedience to His instructions, and to see the blessing of His delivering power. Moses was used in miraculous ways to free the people from slavery and bring them to a promised land.

Conclude by explaining that nothing could destroy God's purposes for Moses. God used everything that Moses went through as preparation for the task He had planned for Moses all along: to be the deliverer of His people and lead them from bondage to freedom. Moses finally saw that God's will had to be done God's way.

APPLY

Option 1: Clear the Pipes. For this option, you need two 10- to 12-inch pieces of pipe, one clogged up and one completely open, and several 2-inch to 3-inch segments of pipe (any kind will do) to give out to students. Ask a local hardware store for scraps or inexpensive suggestions.

Begin by reminding students that Moses wasn't an effective conduit for God's power at first. Hold up the clogged pipe and explain that in Egypt Moses' presumption and anger clogged up the flow of God's power. He had to be emptied of his own pride so that God's power could flow through him. Being rejected by his people and chased out of the country for murder went a long way in dismantling his self-sufficiency. Hold up the clear piece of pipe and explain that in the desert Moses came to understand that while God uses people, it is still He alone who saves. It's *all* about Him!

Give students the small pieces of pipe and have them quietly think about attitudes that may be clogging their own "pipes." Pride? Self-sufficiency? Fear? What is it that keeps them from being an open channel for God to use to His glory? Next, have the group spend some time in "clearing out the pipes" in prayer so that His power can flow mightily through each of them. Encourage them to take their pipes home and place them as a reminder to keep their hearts and minds unclogged and ready for use.

Option 2: Excuses, Excuses. For this option, you need copies of "Excuses, Excuses" (found on the next page) and pens or pencils. Begin by reminding students that when God spoke to Moses from a burning bush, Moses' response was not "Wow, Lord, whatever You say!" but rather "What? Are You serious? Me?" Moses' reticence and timidity resisted God's command and he gave God an excuse for everything!

Handout "Excuses, Excuses" and pens or pencils and have students consider the excuses they give God for not trusting and obeying Him. Then have them consider what God would say about their excuses. The students may not be able to come up with what God would say, so be available to help out. It's important to avoid any sense of judgment and condemnation. The goal is to help students see that God is on their side, working in them, to make them strong and faithful followers. He will supply whatever they need by His own power and wisdom because He wants them to succeed.

When students are finished, ask for volunteers to share what they wrote, and then spend time praying together for greater courage to obey when God speaks. If no one wants to share, then lead the discussion with general excuses people make such as fear, laziness, selfishness, and so forth. Basically, share the things we all deal with and encourage students to band together in God's grace and become people who faithfully follow Him.

Youth Leader Tip

Use everyday words and phrases when you pray, and keep prayers relatively short. Students will feel less pressure and more open to praying themselves when they can relate to how you express yourself.

EXCUSES, EXCUSES

Moses' Excuse	God's Response
The Israelites won't believe that You sent me!	I will do signs and wonders through you so that they will see I am the one working through you.
I can't speak well!	I will send your brother Aaron to help you speak to Pharaoh.

My Excuses	God's Response

REFLECT

The following short devotions are for the students to reflect on and answer during the week. You can make a copy of these pages and distribute to your class or download and print from **www.gospellight.com/uncommon/jh_ the_old_testament.zip**.

1—FREEDOM!

Look up these Bible verses and note *why* God wanted His people to be freed.

❏ Exodus 5:1: "Let my people go that they may _____."
❏ Exodus 7:16: "Let my people go that they may _____."
❏ Exodus 8:1: "Let my people go that they may _____."
❏ Exodus 8:20: "Let my people go that they may _____."

God delivered His people so that they could be free to *worship Him*. The story of Exodus is not just freedom *from* something; it's freedom *to* something. What does it mean to worship God? How do you worship God in your daily life?

_____

_____

_____

What are some of the things God has delivered you *from*? What are some things God has delivered you *to*?

_____

_____

_____

Write a prayer of worship to the Lord below, thanking Him for delivering you!

_____

_____

_____

2—SET APART

Check out Colossians 3:12-17 to see what it means to be set apart for God.
   While the first part of the book of Exodus tells how God delivered the Israelites from Egypt, the last part of the book focuses on the laws God wanted

them to follow. God wanted His people to be *holy,* or set apart for a specific use. And that's just what He did: He set the Israelites apart from their old way of life so they could live the way He wanted.

Picture it this way: If you opened a bag of M&Ms, dumped them on the table, and then separated all the green ones into a pile, you would be making them "holy," because you are setting them apart. The same goes for us. If we have been saved, then God has set us apart. He has delivered us and set us apart so we can live the way He intends us to live.

Read Colossians 3:12-17. What does someone who is "set apart" look like?

_____

_____

_____

_____

Which of these do you see more often in your life? Which do you see less often?

_____

_____

_____

_____

Today, ask God to help you live the holy life He intended you to live.

3—GOD ROCKS!

To find out how Moses and the Israelites praised God after He delivered them, check out Exodus 15:1-5.

The song in this passage is a giant shout of "You rock!" to God. The Israelites describe the Lord as a strong warrior who totally crushed the Egyptian army. God acted with awesome glory to bring His people out of slavery. God doesn't want His people to be slaves to anything—except a grateful love for Him!

What is one area in your life where you need God to deliver you?

_____

_____

_____

_____

Look back through Exodus 15:1-18 and write down any words or phrases about the power of God that stand out to you.

_____

_____

_____

_____

Today, say a prayer to the Mighty God, the great I AM, asking Him to bring you total freedom in that area of your life. He can—and He will!

4—UNFAILING LOVE

Check out Exodus 15:13 to hear what Moses and Miriam had to say about God's love.

Notice the phrase "unfailing love" at the beginning of the verse. This word is translated differently in different versions of the Bible, but it can best be described as a loyal, steadfast, merciful love toward someone who needs help. This is the kind of love that God had toward the Israelites. And this is the kind of love God has for us as well. Let's look at other ways this word is used in the Bible to describe God's love.

Read 1 Chronicles 16:34. How is God's love described?

_____

_____

_____

_____

_____

Look up Jeremiah 31:3. How is God's love described here?

_____

_____

_____

_____

_____

Always remember that God's love is steadfast and eternal. He will *always* love you and *always* lead to you to freedom when you trust Him!

SAMUEL: OBEYING GOD'S VOICE

THE BIG IDEA

Learning to recognize and obey God's voice helps you hear from Him.

SESSION AIMS

In this session you will guide students to (1) listen for and pay attention to God's voice; (2) feel excitement and awe as they realize that God speaks to them and has important things for them to do; and (3) act by obeying God by doing one specific thing they feel He is telling them to do.

THE BIGGEST VERSE

"The Lord came and stood there, calling as at the other times, 'Samuel! Samuel!' Then Samuel said, 'Speak, for your servant is listening'" (1 Samuel 3:10).

OTHER IMPORTANT VERSES

Genesis 41:1-40; Exodus 3:1-15; 20:12; Numbers 22:21-34; 1 Samuel 3:1–4:1; 8:1-3; 2 Samuel 12:1-20; Psalms 19; 99:6; Matthew 5:27-30; 6:3-4; Luke 6:31; 10:27; John 10:2-5,11,14; Acts 9:1-6; Romans 1:18-20; Ephesians 4:29; Revelation 1:1-2

Note: Additional options and worksheets in 8$^1/_2$" x 11" format for this session are available for download at **www.gospellight.com/uncommon/jh_the_old_testament.zip**.

STARTER

Option 1: Listening Quiz. For this option, you will need paper, pens or pencils, small prizes and one of your favorite children's stories, such as the Dr. Seuss classic *Horton Hears a Who*. (For an alternate option, instead of reading the children's story, get a can of Spam and read the ingredients and advertising on the label. Give a prize for a correct response to the pop quiz you are about to give, and give the can of Spam to the person who correctly answers the most questions.)

Introduce this step by explaining that today you are going to read from one of your favorite childhood stories. After you read the story, surprise the students by announcing a pop quiz. After the moaning subsides, distribute the paper and pens or pencils and ask detailed questions about the story, such as, "What was the name of the first person Horton met?" (If you go with the Spam option, ask questions such as, "What was the first ingredient I read?" "Who is the manufacturer?" "What is the net weight of this can of Spam?") Award prizes for correct answers.

Ask the group how they might have listened differently if (1) they had known they were going to be tested on what they were hearing, and (2) what they would have done differently if they had known you were giving prizes for correct answers. Explain that often there are rewards for doing the hard work of listening, especially if we're trying to listen to the right voices. Today, we're going to check out someone who was about their age when he learned that listening to the right voice might be hard work, but it really pays off.

Option 2: Team Telephone. For this option, you will need one lollipop per student. Ahead of time, write a different two- to three-sentence paragraph for every 8 to 10 students. For example: "The cowboys drove their herd through the dusty, red plains of Texas until they came to the bank of the river. There they made camp and enjoyed their first bath in weeks. Little did they know the surprises that lay ahead on the trail."

Youth Leader Tip

Integrating food into your sessions creates an environment where church is associated with fun and enjoyment. The more they enjoy church, the more they will begin to associate God with fun and good times.

Greet students, and then divide the group into teams of 8 to 10 each. (*Note*: If the group is smaller than eight students, use the good old "students vs. adults" standby. Large groups that make up more than three teams can have more than one team at a time playing.) Explain that today the group is going to play Team Telephone. When it's each team's turn, they will stand in a line and you will whisper a paragraph to the first person in line. That person will whisper the paragraph as accurately as possible to the next person, and so on until the information is whispered to the last person. The last person in line will then share with the group the message that he or she heard. An important rule: No repeating the information—what they hear the first time is what they get!

Here's the trick: The other team(s) will be trying to distract them as they are whispering the story down the line. The other teams can do anything verbal—yelling, screaming, talking—to distract the students from listening to what's being whispered in their ear. Also, while they are in line, they will each get a lollipop that *must* stay in their mouth as they whisper the information to the next person.

Following the game, discuss what made listening to each other person easy and what made it difficult. Transition to the next step by explaining that although listening to anyone—including God—often requires work, it is important that we learn to listen to Him so that we can know how He wants us to act. Today, we're going to check out someone who was just about their age when he learned this in an unforgettable way.

MESSAGE

Option 1: A Voice in the Night. For this option, you will need your Bible, pillows, blankets and a chair.

Ask for a show of hands from students who didn't get enough sleep last night. (There should be plenty of hands, since you are dealing with teens!) Select one of those students to come forward to play the role of Samuel, and then choose two volunteers to play the roles of Eli and God. Have the student who is playing the part of God stand on the chair as he or she delivers the messages, and give the student playing the part of Samuel the pillows and blankets.

Explain that while you are reading 1 Samuel 3:1-21, the actors are to act out their roles. Encourage the volunteers to ham it up when they act, and each time they have a line of dialogue they can either mouth the words as you read them or repeat after you when you've finished their line (knowing junior-highers' short memories and attention spans, the longer the line, the better it is to have them just mouth the words as you read them).

After you've read the passage, thank the actors for their performances and discuss the following:

- Have you ever been awakened in the middle of the night? How did you feel? (*Confused, disoriented, groggy.*)
- How do you think Samuel felt when God woke him up? (*Confused, disoriented, groggy.*)
- Who helped Samuel figure out what was happening? (*Eli the priest. This is a good example of the importance of asking others to help us understand what's happening when we think God might be speaking to us.*)
- Why was Samuel reluctant to tell Eli what God was saying? (*Because God told Samuel some pretty bad news about Eli—that he had failed as a father.*)
- How did Eli respond? (*Although the news was painful, he acknowledged God's sovereignty and goodness.*)
- What happened to Samuel as he became an adult? (*He became a prophet—a messenger of God.*)
- What might have been different if he hadn't responded to God's voice and obeyed Him? (*He might never have developed the habit of listening to God and he wouldn't have been able to share God's messages, and he might not have become one of the greatest prophets in all of Israel.*)

Option 2: Phone Call. For this option, you will need your Bible and two cell phones. Ahead of time, ask a parent or other adult to attend the session. Arrange a cue for that person to step out of the room unnoticed and call you on the cell phone a minute or two after you have finished the first step below.

Begin by explaining how important it is to listen and pay attention when someone is speaking to us. Cue the adult volunteer, and then stall until you hear the cell phone ring. At that point, apologize to the group for the interruption and greet the caller: "Oh, hi, Aunt Debbie [or perhaps use your senior pastor's name]." From this point on, the students will only hear and see your end of the conversation, so hone your acting skills to convince them it's a real call.

Make it obvious that you are not really paying attention to what the caller is telling you by rolling your eyes, tapping your feet and periodically whispering statements like, "I'm almost done," and, "yak, yak, yak," to the group. Keep saying things to the caller such as, "Yes, I got it" and "Right, I'm writing down the number," even though you're *not* writing anything down. After about 30 seconds, act surprised and say, "You want me to repeat the number to make sure I got it right? Well, to tell you the truth, I didn't really write it down." Act embarrassed, apologize to the caller for your carelessness, and hang up.

After the call, explain to the students how embarrassed you are and discuss the following questions:

- Have you ever been in a similar situation?
- How did you feel when it became obvious you hadn't been listening?
- What would I have needed to do to really listen? (*Shift my attention from the group to the call, and actually write down the information.*)
- What might happen if you don't listen when someone is speaking to you? (*He or she might get angry at you, or you might miss out on something really important.*)

Finally, expose the call for what it really was—a pretend conversation—and explain that this was one example of how important it is to really listen to people. Explain that today we are going to look at a teenager from the Bible who learned to listen a lot better than you just did now on the phone. Now ask for volunteers to read 1 Samuel 3:1-21 aloud, and discuss the following:

- Why do you think God chose to speak to young Samuel rather than someone older? (*Because Samuel was young, he was probably willing to learn to listen to God's voice. Perhaps being young, Samuel didn't have as many distractions. He might have been more spiritually sensitive.*)
- Why do you think Samuel didn't recognize God's voice? (*No one had taught him what God's voice was like. He didn't realize that God might want to speak personally to him.*)
- Why was Samuel reluctant to tell Eli what God had told him? (*God told him some pretty bad news about Eli—that he had failed as a father.*)
- How did Eli respond? (*Although the news was painful, he acknowledged God's sovereignty and goodness.*)
- What happened once Samuel learned to listen to God? (*God gave him an important message to pass along and began speaking to him more often about other things. Eventually Samuel became known for his close relationship to God; see Psalm 99:6.*)[1]

DIG

Option 1: Ways to Communicate. For this option, you will need several Bibles. Ahead of time, write the following Scripture references on six index cards, one on each card:

- Genesis 41:1-40: Joseph understanding God through dreams
- Exodus 3:1-15: Moses hearing God speak from a burning bush
- Numbers 22:21-34: Balaam hearing from his donkey
- 2 Samuel 12:1-20: David hearing from Nathan
- Acts 9:1-6: Saul hearing from God
- Revelation 1:1-2: John receiving a vision from the Lord

Begin by explaining that God spoke in a pretty incredible way to Samuel, but Samuel is not the only person to have such an amazing encounter with God. Divide students into six groups and distribute the index cards. Instruct them to brainstorm how each story might look if it were written today. Tell the students that they will be performing a short drama to illustrate their ideas about how God might speak to someone today based on the specific example found in their assigned Scripture passage. For example, in the story of Samuel, they might interpret Samuel as getting confused and thinking he hears his radio that he had left on when he fell asleep. Allow a few minutes of planning, and then have each group perform their drama.

After all the groups have performed, ask the group if they think that God still speaks in these ways today. Why or why not? (*God can still speak in the ways that He always has because He never loses His ability to communicate.*) Conclude by discussing (1) how God usually speaks to Christians these days, and (2) in what ways they have experienced God speaking to them.

Option 2: God's Messengers. For this option, you will need nothing but your good looks (and this great book)! Share the following story:

> You and your family live where floods are common, but your dad never lets the dangers of a flood worry him because he believes that God will protect him. During one particularly heavy season of rain, your town is being evacuated because it looks like the whole town is going to be flooded. Your dad tells the policeman who comes to warn you, "Don't worry, God is looking out for us."
>
> Sure enough, the flood comes and forces you and your family to the second story of your home. A National Guardsman comes by in a

boat and yells for you and your family to get in and ride to safety, but your dad simply replies, "Don't worry, God is looking out for us."

The flooding continues, and your family is forced to climb onto the roof of the house. Just as you are clinging to the chimney, a helicopter comes and lowers a rope. But your dad waves it off, saying, "Don't worry, God is looking out for us." By now, you and your family are wet, cold and scared.

Discuss the following questions based on this story:

- What would you tell your dad right about now? (*God is looking out for us by sending the policeman, the National Guardsman and the helicopter pilot. He's speaking and working through them!*)

- Why do you think your dad doesn't recognize God's messengers? (*He doesn't expect God to speak to him through other people. He has a limited understanding of how God speaks and provides for us.*)

- In what ways did God speak to people in the Bible? (*In all sorts of ways: a voice, angels, prayer, Scripture, dreams and circumstances.*)

- In what ways does God speak to us today? (*Most often through prayer, Scripture, fellow Christians, circumstances and an inner urging, but God can—and does—use other means such as dreams, angels, visions and audible voices.*)

- What should we do when we hear God's voice? (*Give God our full attention and obey whatever He commands.*)

- What do we do if we're not sure whether it's God or not? (*Just as Samuel sought out the advice of Eli, we can seek out advice from other adults and friends who have a close relationship with God.*)

Youth Leader Tip

When using an illustration, use true stories about yourself or someone else. It is okay to fool them for a few minutes, but it is best to let them in on the gag before you end the session. Being truthful will help your students trust what you are teaching.

Conclude by reading John 10:2-5,11,14. Point out that when we have a relationship with Jesus, we will recognize when He speaks to us. Another test for whether or not God is really speaking to us is to ask if what we are "hearing" agrees with God's Word, the Bible.

APPLY

Option 1: New Numbers. For this option, you will need several sets of dice, copies of "New Numbers" (found on the following page), and pens or pencils. (*Note*: If you are reluctant to use dice at church, have students individually pick a number between one and six before they look at the handout.)

Distribute "New Numbers" and pens or pencils, and then divide students into groups of four or five. Give each group one die and explain that each person in the group will roll the die and check off the corresponding Scripture passage on his or her handout. (If you are having students just pick numbers, the passage would correspond to whatever number they chose.) When everyone has rolled, allow a few minutes for students to complete the handouts, and ask them to share their responses.

Close by praying that God will give students the strength and desire to obey Him by doing the things He has told them to do.

Option 2: Ears Wide Open. For this option, you will need copies of "Ears Wide Open" (found on pages 124-125) and pens or pencils. Ahead of time, arrange for two or three adults to help keep track of students while they are outside completing the handout.

Explain that now that we've seen how God spoke to Samuel through a voice he could actually hear, as well as all the other ways God spoke to people in the Bible, we're going to take a few minutes to let God speak to us. Distribute "Ears Wide Open" and pens or pencils. Explain that the group is going to have 15 minutes to work through this handout and see what God might be saying to them. Ask adult volunteers to lead students to a large open area such as a lawn or picnic area where they can spread out and work through the handout independently.

After a few minutes, call everyone together. Invite those who feel comfortable about what they wrote to share with the group. (Let students know that it's okay not to share.) Allow time for sharing, and then close in prayer asking that God would give the students ears wide open to hear Him this week.

Ðew Ðumbers

Name: _____   Date: _____

Circle the number of the command from God that you have been assigned for the week.

1. "Honor your father and your mother" (Exodus 20:12).

2. Run away from lust and flee temptation (see Matthew 5:27-30).

3. "When you give to the needy, do not let your left hand know what your right hand is doing, so that your giving may be in secret" (Matthew 6:3-4).

4. "Do to others as you would have them do to you" (Luke 6:31).

5. "Love your neighbor as yourself" (Luke 10:27).

6. "Don't use bad language. Say only what is good and helpful to those you are talking to, and what will give them a blessing" (Ephesians 4:29, *TLB*).

Read the Scripture passage next to the number you circled and ask God how He wants you to obey Him this week, and then write down what you believe He is asking you to do.

_____

_____

_____

_____

Write down what you need from God in order to obey what He is asking you to do, and then pray that He will use you to bless others and become more like Jesus.

_____

_____

_____

_____

EARS WIDE OPEN

Ask God to speak to you through the following passage from Psalm 40:1-8, and then answer the questions on the next page.

I waited and waited and waited for GOD.
At last he looked; finally he listened.
He lifted me out of the ditch, pulled me from deep mud.
He stood me up on a solid rock to make sure I wouldn't slip.
He taught me how to sing the latest God-song,
a praise-song to our God.
More and more people are seeing this: they enter the mystery,
abandoning themselves to GOD.

Blessed are you who give yourselves over to GOD,
turn your backs on the world's "sure thing,"
ignore what the world worships;
The world's a huge stockpile of GOD-wonders and God-thoughts.
Nothing and no one comes close to you!
I start talking about you, telling what I know,
and quickly run out of words.
Neither numbers nor words account for you.
Doing something for you, bringing something to
you—that's not what you're after.
Being religious, acting pious—that's not
what you're asking for.
You've opened my ears so I can listen.

So I answered, "I'm coming. I read in your letter
what you wrote about me,
And I'm coming to the party you're throwing for me."
That's when God's Word entered my life,
became part of my very being (THE MESSSAGE).

Do you feel a little like you're in a ditch right now? If so, what do you need to ask God to do to lift you out of it?

_____

_____

_____

_____

_____

What would it mean for you to fully give yourself over to God this week?

_____

_____

_____

_____

_____

What is God looking to do in your life?

_____

_____

_____

_____

_____

God is throwing you a party. What's it like? What keeps you from going?

_____

_____

_____

_____

_____

How can you let God's Word enter your life and become a part of all you are this week?

_____

_____

_____

_____

_____

REFLECT

The following short devotions are for the students to reflect on and answer during the week. You can make a copy of these pages and distribute to your class or download and print from **www.gospellight.com/uncommon/jh_ the_old_testament.zip.**

1—WAITING FOR THE CALL

Flip to Habakkuk 2:1 to figure out where you should be stationing yourself!

If you were waiting for your best friend to call you any minute and tell you about a really cool party later that evening, where would you wait for the call?

- ❏ On the big couch in the TV room while watching a movie with surround sound
- ❏ In front of a computer, playing a game
- ❏ Standing around as you are texting another friend
- ❏ In the basement while playing a noisy video game
- ❏ In a chair right by the phone

Sometimes waiting for God's instructions is like waiting for a phone call. It is easy to miss what God is saying if we're too busy listening to other things. Even if it seems boring or pointless, waiting quietly for God is really worthwhile if we're serious about knowing what He wants for us.

What kind of "noise" could be preventing you from hearing God's voice?

_____

_____

_____

_____

Ask God today to help you to get rid of that noise and keep your antennae pointed toward Him.

2—ALL TALK?

Try to find Psalm 37:7 with your eyes closed.

Gabby Gabberino loved to talk and talk and talk. She talked so much in class that she had to sit at a desk right beside her teacher, Mr. Blank, so he could keep an eye on her. She talked so much during lunch period that she never finished the lunch her mom packed for her. She came home from school, got on the phone and talked and talked and talked to her friends, forgetting dinner, her homework and even her favorite television shows.

When you pray, are you all talk like Gabby, or do you ever sit quietly and see if God has anything to say to you? Try it today, if you haven't before. You may be pleasantly surprised!

3—FOLLOWING JESUS' MODEL

Flip to Luke 5:15-16 to see what Jesus would do.

Imagine that you needed to study for a big test. Where would be the best place to do so? When would be the best time to study?

- ❑ In the living room, during commercials between your favorite show
- ❑ In your best friend's bedroom, while she plays loud video games
- ❑ In the grocery store, sprawled out in the middle of the ice cream aisle
- ❑ In your bedroom, under a bright lamp at your desk

Just like studying for a big test, having a relationship with God often requires time and a quiet place to pray. Time with God is important, but when you just "squeeze it in," you don't get all you could be getting out of it! Follow Jesus' model and make time to spend with God the Father.

Every night this week, think about the next day and see when you can set aside a small chunk of time to spend with Him. It will be worth it!

4—SHHHH!

Read Psalm 16:7-8 and get some instructions!

At night Griffin has to do his homework, but it doesn't take much time. Sometimes after that he plays video games, goes on the Internet or reads a comic book, but mostly he just watches TV and sits around, eating chips, drinking soda and talking to his friends on the phone. Sometimes when he goes to church he hears his pastor talk about having a quiet time with God. Griffin thinks to himself, *It's such a hassle, and I don't have the time. What good is it anyway?*

A quiet time is important because it's easier to pay attention to God and re-member Him when you're spending time together every day. Do you have a quiet time with God every day? If so, what do you do?

_____

_____

_____

_____

Do you read your Bible regularly during your quiet time? Pray?

_____

_____

_____

_____

If you don't have a quiet time with God, why not? Does it sound too boring or hard?

_____

_____

_____

_____

This week, consider spending seven minutes with God every day. Caution: If you do, it might just become a habit!

DAVID: SEEKING AFTER GOD'S HEART

THE BIG IDEA

David focused his trust on God no matter what he faced, and this made him a man after God's heart.

SESSION AIMS

In this session you will guide students to (1) explore some of the ups and downs of David's life; (2) realize that David kept his focus on God no matter what; and (3) be encouraged to pursue a similar life of faith.

THE BIGGEST VERSE

"I have found David son of Jesse a man after my own heart; he will do everything I want him to do" (Acts 13:22).

OTHER IMPORTANT VERSES

1 Samuel 6:1-19; 16:1-13,23; 17; 19:12-18; 23:2,4,14; 24; 25:29; 26; 30:8; 2 Samuel 2:1; 5:1-5,19,23; 11; 12:1-25; Psalms 6; 24; 51; 119:105; Isa. 64:4; Lamentations 3:26; Matthew 6:33

Note: Additional options and worksheets in 8$^1/_2$" x 11" format for this session are available for download at **www.gospellight.com/uncommon/jh_the_old_testament.zip**.

STARTER

Option 1: The Hand Is Quicker Than the Eye. For this option, you will need a ping-pong ball, three identical cups (not glass), a table, lively background music and prizes. Ahead of time, place the cups upside down on a table. You'll be moving the cups around in the old-fashioned, "the hand is quicker than the eye" carnival game, so practice being fast and tricky!

Welcome students and ask for a volunteer. Have him or her step up to the front and watch while you place the ping-pong ball under one of the cups. Then explain that you will be moving the cups around trying to make him or her lose track of the ball. The volunteer's job is to keep his or her eye focused on the cup with the ball under it the whole time so that he or she knows where it is when you're finished. If the volunteer can tell you where it is, he or she wins. If the volunteer can't, he or she loses.

Play the game a few times, inviting new volunteers to join the game. Have lively background music playing while you're mixing the cups to add to the festivities (and distraction!). Give out prizes to winning volunteers.

Wrap things up by explaining that what we focus on makes a huge difference in our lives. From simple things like watching cups being moved around to big things like pursuing God and His will for us, when we fix our attention on something, we begin to know it and it begins to change us. King David was a man who fixed his attention on God—through amazing victories and humiliating defeats—and that constant focus helped David know God and learn to trust Him regardless of the circumstances. This made him a man with a great faith and remarkable love for God.

Option 2: Ping-Pong Spectacle. For this option, you will need a ping-pong table, a ping-pong ball, four ping-pong paddles and four strong prescription eyeglasses (these can be real eyewear that you borrow or find at a thrift store, 3-D movie eyewear, prop glasses smeared with petroleum jelly—anything that keeps the volunteers from being able to clearly focus). Ahead of time, set up the table where students will watch the match.

Welcome everyone and ask for four ping-pong aficionados. Get volunteers set up with paddles and a ball, and just as you signal the start of the game, suddenly stop and announce that you forgot their special eye gear. Give each player a pair of glasses to wear, and then start the game. Hopefully, your students will create a wonderfully amusing spectacle (pun intended!) as they attempt to generate a volley that lasts more than three seconds. After a few minutes, change players if your students are up for the challenge.

Close the game by explaining that being able to focus on something is the key to success. As our ping-pong aficionados proved, unless we have clear vision, we may misjudge things despite out best efforts. King David was a man who maintained clear sight on God no matter what was going on around him. Through amazing victories and humiliating defeats, that constant focus helped David know God and learn to trust Him, which made him a man with a great faith and remarkable love for God.

MESSAGE

Option 1: Seeing Clearly. For this option, you will need Bibles and as many binoculars as you can get. One per student would be ideal. (Time to contact the local Boy Scouts!)

Begin by explaining that one of the most well known Old Testament characters is David, the shepherd-turned-king. Explain that David was truly remarkable in many ways—some good and some bad. He was a handsome man, a prolific poet, a skilled musician, a brave warrior, a beloved king—as well as a selfish liar, a deliberate murderer, and a calculating adulterer. But the one thing that makes him a model for believers today is the way he kept his focus on God no matter what was going on in his life. David focused on God, and that sustained him throughout his life.

Impress the idea that when we focus on God, not ourselves, we have a perspective that will carry us through everything that we face, and David gives us great examples of this principle. Hand out the binoculars to students and ask them to look through them at items on the opposite side of your meeting area—anything far away. Ask them to locate one object and then blur the focus in and out. Have them describe what it feels like to watch things go from unfocused to focused (for instance, first frustration then peace, first confusion then clarity, and so forth). Next, ask them to describe the way in which the lenses enhance even 20/20 vision (for example, greater clarity or

Youth Leader Tip

Participation is an important ingredient for a successful youth meeting. Object lessons provide great opportunities for memorable interaction and discussion that will get your students thinking.

great detail). Connect to the main idea of the message by explaining that, like David, when we keep a clear focus on God—His power, His timing, and His forgiveness—we see life with greater clarity and detail, which enables us to live with the right perspective.

Collect the binoculars and distribute the Bibles. Explain to the group that first we need to focus on *God's power.* Have students open to 1 Samuel 17. Set up the context of the passage by explaining that, at this point, David is a teenager but has just been anointed by the prophet Samuel, which means that someday David will be king. Right now, however, he is still taking care of his father's sheep and running supplies out to his brothers who are serving in the Israelite army. The Israelites, under the leadership of King Saul, are facing one of their most powerful enemies: the Philistines.[1] Now read the passage and have the students follow along. (*Note:* This takes 5 to 7 minutes without stopping, but it's an engaging narrative, so have fun with it!)

After reading the story, explain that it would have been easy for David to focus on his own abilities—especially since he had just been told that God would make him a king—but instead he focused on God's power rather than his own. Reread verses 45 to 47. Note that it would also have been easy for David to focus on the giant in front of him, but instead, he kept his sight fixed on the One whose power was greater than an extremely tall, fully armored, defiant beast of a warrior. That right perspective allowed David to see the God who had always defended him and would, for His glory, defend him again now. David's sight was on God's power, not his enemy's.

Continue by stating that next we need to focus on *God's timing.* Have students follow along as a volunteer reads aloud 1 Samuel 16:1-13. Explain that David was somewhere around 15 when these events occurred, and then instruct the group to flip page by page through 1 Samuel until they reach the end. State that *years* pass—most of which David spends fleeing an angry king, living in foreign lands and hiding in caves—and he is *still* not king! But David never once worries or gets upset about this, because he keeps his focus on God's timing, not his own.

Ask students to flip page by page to 2 Samuel 5 and follow along as a volunteer reads verses 1 to 5 aloud. Explain that it took about 15 years for God's promise of kingship to be fulfilled in David's life. At least twice David had perfect and completely legitimate opportunities to take things into his own hands and become the king, but he didn't.[2] He was content to wait for God to act on his behalf. David kept his focus on God's timing, and that perspective kept him faithfully content.

Explain that the third thing we need to focus on is *God's forgiveness.* After David had been king for a while, he made a huge mistake. Have students turn to 2 Samuel 11:1-26 and follow along as a volunteer reads the passage aloud. God had given David everything he could have wanted—land, family, favor, wealth—but somehow David lost perspective and chose to sin. However, David faced the consequences of his sin, and he didn't lose sight of the greatness of God and His forgiveness. Keeping his eyes on God's forgiveness enabled David to repent and find redemption.

Explain that sometimes our faith can feel disqualified by our failures. When we sin, we may want to take our focus off God because of our shame—but that's the opposite of what we should do. While sin displeases God, it never dilutes His goodness, grace or love. So, even in our failures, if we keep our eyes on God, we can realize that we have hope in His redemption. Have a volunteer read aloud 2 Samuel 12:1-23 while the rest of the group follows along. Draw their attention to verse 13. When confronted, David acknowledged his sin, and God took it away. This shows us that when we make a mistake and sin, we must keep our focus on God and His forgiveness—not on ourselves and our bad choices. God is bigger than all our mistakes.

Conclude by reiterating the main idea of this section: David's consistent focus on God's power, timing and forgiveness sustained him throughout his entire life. Focusing on God leads to faithful trust because it allows us to see who He is and then who we are. When we see Him first, we keep the right perspective of ourselves.

Option 2: Faith Mural. For this option you will need Bibles, butcher paper, poster paint and brushes (or broad-tipped markers) and masking tape. Ahead of time, lay a long strip of butcher paper on the floor where students can get to it easily. Make sure the paint or brushes are ready to use.

Begin by explaining that the group will be looking at the life of David to see how his steady focus on God—His power, His timing and His forgiveness—enabled him to live from a right perspective and cultivate a confident trust in the Lord. Hand out Bibles and have students get into three groups. Each group will work on one of the stories listed below. Instruct the groups that their job is to read the passage, discuss the events and how David's focus on God sustained him, and then use the paints or markers to create a mural of that scene, which they will explain to the rest of the group. (*Note:* This activity puts the bulk of the work on the students, so be sure to move around the room and offer your help and guidance. As long as the students can draw out the main facts about the story, you can augment their explanation of how David's focus on God brought him through.)

- **God's Power** (1 Samuel 17:1-58): This is the story of David and Goliath. Most students are probably familiar with this narrative and should be able to work through the content on their own. The main point to help students draw out is that David wasn't focusing on either himself or on the giant he was about to face. David kept his attention on God, and that gave him the right point of view.

- **God's Timing** (1 Samuel 24 and 26): These are the accounts of David sparing Saul's life. It will probably be a more challenging section for students unless you set up the greater context of the events by pointing out that David was around 15 when he was called to be the next king of Israel, but it took about 15 more years before it actually happened. During that time David faced exile, attack, rejection, hunger, treachery, deceit, failure and other difficult situations. The main point to help students draw out is that by refusing to kill Saul and force the prophecy to happen, David demonstrated his faith in God. He kept his focus on God's timing, and that perspective allowed him to live faithfully and contentedly.

- **God's Forgiveness** (2 Samuel 11:1–12:25): This is the story of David and Bathsheba, another narrative with which students will probably be familiar. The main point to help students draw out is that even in deliberate sin, David didn't turn his focus away from God but accepted Nathan's rebuke and repented. David kept God's forgiveness in view rather than his egregious error, and this enabled him to receive redemption. David still faced the consequences of his sin, but he did not let shame keep him from trusting in God.

Once the students have finished the mural, tape it on a wall where everyone can see it. Have student groups take turns explaining the Bible passage and their corresponding artwork. Conclude by reiterating the main idea: David's consistent focus on God—His power, His timing, His forgiveness—sustained him throughout his life. Focusing on God leads to faithful trust because it allows us to see who He is and then who we are. When we see Him first, we keep the right perspective of ourselves.

DIG

Option 1: Sovereign Comfort. For this option, you will need Bibles, a bundle of sticks tied together securely, copies of "Sovereign Comfort" (found on the next page), and pens or pencils.

Explain that one of the ways David was able to have such great faith in God was that he trusted God's sovereignty. Note that "sovereignty" means that God's plans cannot be thwarted for any reason—He always accomplishes His will. Distribute Bibles and copies of "Sovereign Comfort," and instruct students to spend time alone working through the handout. When they are done, gather together and discuss their responses.

To wrap things up, hold up the bundle of sticks as you or a volunteer read aloud 1 Samuel 25:29 and 1 Samuel 23:14. Reinforce the truth that if God has brought us into His family, we can be confident that His sovereignty will sustain us. Impress on the group that rather than being restrictive, God's sovereignty brings abundant comfort because we can know He will do what He has said. There is nothing—not even our failures—that can undermine His divine will. Knowing this allows us to trust God more completely, just as David did.

Option 2: God's Will, God's Way. For this option, you will need Bibles and students who like to talk.

Explain that one of the ways in which David modeled a focused life was that he constantly went to God before he did something to ask what should be done and how it should be accomplished. Even when an action or response made sense to him, he first went to God to get the okay. David was interested in doing God's will, God's way.

Distribute Bibles. Have students look up the following verses and take turns reading them aloud: 1 Samuel 23:2; 1 Samuel 23:4; 1 Samuel 30:8; 2 Samuel 2:1; 2 Samuel 5:19; and 2 Samuel 5:23. Explain that in the Old Testament, "to inquire" meant more than just to casually ask. It referred to using an "ephod," which was a tool for purposeful prayer used by a priest in order to find out

Youth Leader Tip

A goal should be to educate your students to read the Bible for themselves. Have them read the verses for you—even if it takes longer. They will learn that the Bible is open and accessible to them.

SOVEREIGN COMFORT

What does it mean that God is sovereign?

_____

_____

_____

Read 2 Samuel 12:7-8. How do you see God's sovereignty in David's life?

_____

_____

_____

Turn to 2 Samuel 7:18-29. How many times does David refer to God as sovereign?

_____

_____

_____

Look up the following verses about God's plans and fill in the blanks:

Psalm 33:11: "But the plans of the LORD _____."

Proverbs 19:21: "Many are the plans in a man's heart, but _____."

Isaiah 55:11: "My word . . . will not return to me empty, but will _____
and achieve _____."

Jeremiah 29:11: "'For I know _____,' declares the LORD, 'plans
to _____, plans to give you _____.'"

Ephesians 1:11: "In him we were also chosen, having been predestined according to the
_____ who works out everything in conformity with
_____."

Does God's sovereignty mean that you have no choices at all? How would you explain the difference
between the two?

_____

_____

_____

After considering these verses, think about how your perspective of God's sovereignty has changed.

God's will in a given situation. Point out that David often was asking not only *what* God wanted him to do, but also *how* He wanted him to do it. Today, we don't need an ephod to hear from God: He has given us His Word and His Spirit. So, for us, inquiring means that we focus on Him through Bible reading and prayer, seeking His will and responding in faithful obedience.

Next, have students discuss the following questions:

- What does David's life suggest about inquiring of, or seeking, God first?

- Does God care about every decision you make? Explain.

- What kinds of things do people rely on in order to make decisions? Which of these are useful and which are not?

- How can you be sure that you're following God's plan and not something you made up yourself?

- Is it possible to do God's will *your* way? Explain.

- In your own experience, what role has God's Word had in your understanding of God's will?

Close by helping students realize that if they want to live a focused, God-honoring life, they must become people who seek His will and His way. Help them see that while this feels counterintuitive in our extremely individualistic society, it is the only way to become a person "after [God's] own heart" (Acts 13:22). When we inquire of God, we are acting in faith: going to God shows that we believe He exists, that we believe He has a plan, and that we believe He will respond to us when we come to Him. It is this that pleases God and brings us into closer communion with Him.

APPLY

Option 1: What Are You After? For this option, you need a Bible. Ahead of time, if you can use PowerPoint, create a slide that reads, "What are you after?"

Pair up students for a game of tag. The object is simple: One person simply chases the other. When someone is "caught," he or she becomes the one chasing. (If you have a large group and not a lot of space, you can just choose to have a couple of volunteers demonstrate the game.) After a few minutes, gather together to talk about chasing and being chased. What was it like? What emotions were engaged? How did it feel to almost catch up with what they were chasing? How did it make a difference when it was someone they knew?

Gather together and remind students that David spent a lot of his life running around from here to there, but there was really only one thing he was chasing: God. David fought *because of his love for God*. David sang *because of his love for God*. David built up a kingdom *because of his love for God*. David was always *after the One he loved*. Read aloud Acts 13:22: "I [God] have found David son of Jesse a man after my own heart; he will do everything I want him to do." Remind students that David's behavior wasn't perfect, but he had the kind of heart that comes from focused attention on the Lord. No matter what he was doing, he was always chasing God.

Have students consider how they would answer the question "What are you after?" (Put up the PowerPoint slide at this point if you made one.) If the students are having a hard time with this, ask them to think about how they spend their time, what matters most to them, on what they base their decisions, or what they spend their time chasing. If they are reticent to talk about themselves, broaden the discussion to general (people today) rather than personal (I) responses.

After the group members have shared some ideas, encourage them to identify one way they can refocus their lives so that they're chasing God more purposefully. Be careful not to make this a guilt session but just a chance for them to reflect on where they are so that they can make changes that bring them closer to God. End by encouraging them with Jesus' promise that when they "seek first the kingdom and his righteousness . . . all these things will be given to [them] as well" (Matthew 6:33). We never give up more than God gives, so no matter what we face, we can keep up the chase.

End in prayer, asking God to continue His sovereign work in the students' lives as He makes them into people who chase after Him.

Option 2: Come into Focus. For this option, you need copies of "Come into Focus" (found on the next page) and pens or pencils.

Explain to students that they have spent most of this lesson talking about the importance of keeping a clear focus on God, so now, you want them to take a few minutes and make it personal. Distribute Bibles, "Come into Focus" handouts and pens or pencils. Have students work alone to complete the handout. After they're finished, regroup and offer them a chance to share their responses. End in prayer, asking God to give the students clear vision that leads to strong faith.

Come into Focus

In the lenses in the glasses below, write down things that you know about God that you can focus on, such as "sovereign," "loving," and so forth. Then, around the glasses, write down things that try to blur your focus on God, such as "fear," "unbelief," and so forth.

Circle the one thing you wrote in the lenses that is the most important to you right now. Why is this so important for you to focus on?

_____

_____

_____

Now circle the one thing you wrote around the glasses that is the most difficult for you right now. How does it blur your vision of God?

_____

_____

_____

David didn't give up, even when things got really bad. Instead, he kept his gaze on the One who had called him and who would deliver him. Write down what you think God would say to encourage you right now about keeping your focus on Him despite what you are going through.

_____

_____

_____

When we focus on God, we have the right point of view, no matter what we're seeing!

REFLECT

The following short devotions are for the students to reflect on and answer during the week. You can make a copy of these pages and distribute to your class or download and print from **www.gospellight.com/uncommon/jh_ the_old_testament.zip.**

1—NOT ALWAYS WHAT IT APPEARS

Have you ever misjudged someone based on appearance? Have you ever been misjudged for the same reason? Then you'll identify with this story! Read 1 Samuel 16:1-13 and find out what happened.

Whom did Samuel think God had chosen? Why? (Look at verse 7.)

_____

_____

_____

_____

How many brothers passed before Samuel (see verses 8-9)? Who was chosen?

_____

_____

_____

_____

Why did God choose this person?

_____

_____

_____

_____

People often get caught up in outward appearances and make judgments based on what they see. They look at age, hair, skin, size and manner to determine whether or not someone is acceptable. But God says He looks deeper than that—He looks into a person's *heart*. He sees who a person is, not just how he or she appears. So spend a minute asking God to help you see others through His perspective. You can't tell just by looking at someone what he or she is actually like!

2—THE POWER OF MUSIC

David was a skilled musician. He wrote tons of songs, and when he played them for King Saul, the "evil spirit" would leave him. Don't believe it? Then read 1 Samuel 16:23.

Music is not only a cool way to pass time, but it's also a powerful tool for shaping our thoughts and influencing our emotions. List the top three songs you've been listening to this week:

_____

_____

_____

_____

_____

Now, next to each title, jot down the basic idea of the lyrics. What is the song about? What does it say?

The music you listen to can influence what you think about. What you think about can influence how you feel. And how you feel can influence what you do. So today, think about your iTunes playlists and your CD collection and ask yourself if it is music that moves you in the right direction.

3—WAIT AND SEE

The lesson this week focused on how long David had to wait for God's promise to actually occur. What's the longest you've waited for something? How did you feel when you finally got it?

_____

_____

_____

_____

_____

What does Isaiah 64:4 say about waiting?

_____

_____

_____

_____

Now look up Lamentations 3:26. What does this passage say about waiting?

_____

_____

_____

Sometimes waiting seems like torture, but it's actually a way we learn to trust. God wants us to become people who believe His Word no matter how long it takes to see it come to pass. So, next time you're waiting, rather than getting impatient and angry, just think of it as a chance to show God that you trust Him. If you wait, you will see!

4—THE SIGHT RESTORER

Quick! Place a check next to any of these situations that you've experienced. Circle the one that limited your sight the most.

- ❑ Lost contacts or glasses
- ❑ Snowstorm
- ❑ Blackout
- ❑ Severe rain
- ❑ Thick fog
- ❑ Dust or dirt in my eye

When our vision is hindered, what's the first thing we do? We stop, right? We immediately try to get our sight back. We instinctively want to see. This holds true in our spiritual lives as well. We are made to "see" God and live with a sense of His presence around us, but many things can blur our focus on God. So, what should you do when your spiritual gaze is dim? You should pull out the ultimate sight restorer: the Bible!

What does Psalm 119:105 say about this?

_____

_____

_____

God has given you a constant means of seeing Him clearly: His Word. So turn on the light more often!

JOSIAH: GETTING RID OF IDOLS

THE BIG IDEA

Getting rid of the idols in your life may require lots of changes.

SESSION AIMS

In this session you will guide students to (1) learn that there are many things that keep them from God; (2) feel hopeful about changes they can make that will help them grow closer to Christ; and (3) act in obedience to the Holy Spirit to get rid of one idol in their lives this week.

THE BIGGEST VERSE

"The king ordered Hilkiah the high priest, the priests next in rank and the door-keepers to remove from the temple of the Lord all the articles made for Baal and Asherah and all the starry hosts. He burned them outside Jerusalem in the fields of the Kidron Valley and took the ashes to Bethel" (2 Kings 23:4).

OTHER IMPORTANT VERSES

Exodus 20:1-5; 2 Kings 22:1–23:30; Matthew 6:24; 1 Corinthians 10:13; Philippians 4:13; James 1:17

Note: Additional options and worksheets in 8^1/$_2$" x 11" format for this session are available for download at **www.gospellight.com/uncommon/jh_the_old_testament.zip**.

STARTER

Option 1: Toss It Out. For this option, you will need several large trash bags, masking tape and a bathroom scale. Ahead of time, use the tape to mark a line on the floor approximately 10 yards from where you plan to instruct the teams to gather.

Greet students, divide them into teams of 8 to 10, and give each team a trash bag. Instruct each team to send the trash bag and two volunteers down to the tape line, and then explain that they will be collecting trash from their team. Clarify that you don't mean real trash but anything that their team is carrying or wearing that could go into the trash bag (jackets, shoes, socks, hair accessories, and such) without unclothing anyone. (*Note:* This game involves tossing items into the trash bag, so instruct students not to "throw away" anything breakable.)

One at a time, have a member from each team come forward to throw an item toward their team's bag. The two team members holding the trash bag may move to position the bags so that items land in them, but they have to return to the tape line before the next team member can throw.

After everyone has tossed his or her "trash," weigh each bag and congratulate the team who threw away the most. Explain that usually the trash we throw out is grosser than this stuff. Today, we're going to look at a type of spiritual trash found in the Bible.

Continue by stating that the word used in the Bible for what we might call spiritual trash is "idol." An idol is anything in which we put our trust (or time, money and energy) apart from God and His Word. In biblical days, people worshiped little carved images of wood and stone representing pagan gods in the hopes of securing a good crop, victory in war, or healing from an illness. Today, idols come in new forms but still draw our trust and focus away from God and fill our lives with garbage. During this session, we will look at a story about a teenager in the Old Testament to help us understand why we need to trash the idols in our lives.

Youth Leader Tip
Involve kids that need help connecting by asking them to help you do the set-up for an activity, keep score, or help pull names if you are doing a drawing. Always remember to praise the student and show appreciation for his or her help!

Option 2: Trashed Out. For this option, you will need just the real-life news story printed below.

Greet students and ask them to turn to the person next to them and share which household chore they hate the most and why. After a minute or two, take an informal poll of the most hated chores. Be sure to ask if anybody included taking out the trash. If nobody mentions this, you might need to check some pulses, and then ask, "So, you all *like* taking out the trash?" When the group protests—and they will—discuss why they don't like it. Ask them what would happen if they didn't ever take out the trash. Next, introduce the following true story about one family who let its trash problem get completely out of hand.

Trashed Out
Couple Relieved by Discovery of Their Dirty Little Secret

When authorities discovered the 33,000 pounds of garbage, trash and human waste in her home, Deborah Eggert said she was "relieved that the nightmare was over." Mrs. Eggert, her husband, Michael, and their four children, ages 2 to 14, had retreated to tiny areas of their five-room home by the time their garbage-packed house and garage in a middle-class neighborhood were uncovered last month.

"I always thought, 'Well, I'll get to it, I'll get to it,'" she said.

A few years ago, Mrs. Eggert said, she began to feel hopeless about ever changing her life. She did less and less housekeeping.

"I guess you kind of get to a point where you give up," Mrs. Eggert said. "I'm having a hard time understanding how it did happen. But I remember feeling there wasn't anything I could do about it. When I went into the house, I just blanked the mess out of my mind."

Now the Eggerts are trying to understand how they allowed their lives to run utterly out of control. In the months before the house was discovered, the entire family slept on a single set of bunk beds. Clean clothes were stored in the closet and stuffed into bureau drawers. A clear path led to the beds through putrid piles of soiled diapers, garbage and plastic bags of trash.

Without running water for the past two years, the Eggerts said, they washed their clothes at a commercial laundry. They carried home jugs of water from a gas station or nearby brewery. They stood in a plastic tub and poured water over themselves to wash. They went to the bathroom in plastic bags.[1]

Ask the group if they could imagine having 33,000 pounds of garbage in their home. They might not believe that their own lives could ever get as messy as that, but even this mess began with just a little trash at first. It can be the same for spiritual trash. Ask for examples of some of the trash in students' lives that God would want them to take out. (You might need to give a few examples such as pornography, bad habits and selfish attitudes.) Continue by stating that the Bible tells us that holding on to garbage of any kind in our lives can have serious consequences. The tricky part is that sometimes we want to keep what the Bible calls trash: idols.

Explain that an idol is anything that we honor and love more than God and His Word. In biblical days (and in many cultures around the world today), people worshiped images of wood and stone representing pagan gods in order to secure a good crop, victory in war or healing from an illness. Those things we honor and love more than God and His Word might come in new forms today, but they still draw our trust and focus away from the Lord and fill our lives with garbage.

Transition to the next section by praying that God would open students' eyes to the dangers of idols.

MESSAGE

Option 1: Dump the Idols. For this option, you will need one copy of "Josiah: The Quick Version" (found on the following page), a whiteboard and a dry-erase marker (or a large posterboard and felt-tip pens).

Divide the group into pairs, and then say something such as, "If you're like me, when you were getting dressed today, you followed a few clothing guidelines, like deciding that you needed to wear two shoes, your belt should go through the loops on your pants and your socks should match." Explain that today you're going to have a contest to see who is the best at breaking the clothing guidelines.

Instruct students to take a quick look at their partners and then stand back-to-back and change something about how they look that violates one of these rules (such as taking off one sock or putting glasses on backward). Tell them not to turn around until you give the signal.

Allow 15 seconds of back-to-back time, and then signal the pairs to face each other again and try to guess what each partner has changed. The first partner in each pair who states what has been changed is the winner; have that person move over to the right side of the room and find another partner. Con-

Josiah: The Quick Version

Condensed from 2 Kings 22–23:30

It had been years since the glorious times of King David. The kingdom of Israel had been divided into two parts: Israel and Judah. At this time, they were both under the authority and rule of the Assyrians.

At the young age of eight, Josiah was crowned king of Judah after his father had been as-sassinated. Years later, as he became more interested in the faith and ways of his ancestors, Josiah sent one of his servants to provide supplies for the rebuilding of the Temple in Jerusalem. While the workers began their renovations, they discovered a copy of the Scriptures and brought it to their king. "When the king heard the words of the Book of the Law, he tore his robes" (2 Kings 22:11)—a symbol of his sorrow.

Josiah realized that he and the people of Judah had strayed far from God's laws by wor-shiping idols and following other gods, so he immediately sent his servants and priests to ask God what he should do. His servants found a prophetess through whom God sent the follow-ing message: "I am going to bring disaster on this place and its people, according to everything written in the book the king of Judah has read. Because they have forsaken me and burned in-cense to other gods and provoked me to anger by all the idols their hands have made, my anger will burn against this place and will not be quenched" (2 Kings 22:16-17).

Then God also said, "Because your heart was responsive and you humbled yourself be-fore the LORD when you heard what I have spoken against this place and its people, that they would become accursed and laid waste, and because you tore your robes and wept in my pres-ence, I have heard you, declares the LORD. Therefore I will gather you to your fathers, and you will be buried in peace. Your eyes will not see all the disaster I am going to bring on this place" (2 Kings 22:19-20).

Following these words from God, Josiah gathered all the people of his kingdom and read to them the Book of the Covenant that had been found. When he had finished reading, Josiah renewed the covenant to the Lord and vowed to obey with all his heart and soul the things that had been commanded. Then the people of Judah pledged themselves to the covenant (see 2 Kings 23:1-3) and Josiah ordered a massive, kingdom-wide spiritual cleansing, removing idols from places of worship and breaking and burning them.

He also stopped the evil practices associated with idol worship by killing the priests of the false gods so that they would not lead people astray again. Finally, Josiah ordered the celebra-tion of the Passover in Jerusalem, which was something that had been forgotten for generations.

Because of his commitment to God and his commitment to rid his kingdom of idols, Josiah is remembered in Scripture in this way: "Neither before nor after Josiah was there a king like him who turned to the LORD as he did—with all his heart and with all his soul and with all his strength, in accordance with all the Law of Moses" (2 Kings 23:25). Josiah reigned for 31 years before he was killed in battle with the Egyptians, and the consequences of Israel's past sins began to catch up with its people.

tinue the contest, moving winners over to the right until you have only two contestants left for the championship round.

After the winner has been decided, explain that when we break simple clothing guidelines, there's usually not much of a consequence (other than looking slightly foolish). However, there are other rules that carry much more serious consequences when they're broken. A young teen named Josiah learned what can happen when you break God's rules.

Read "Josiah: The Quick Version" aloud, and then discuss the following questions, writing each of the students' responses on the whiteboard:

- How might Josiah have felt when he realized that his people had been breaking God's rules? (*He probably felt ashamed of his kingdom and remorseful for how far they had moved from God, but he also must have had hope, since he had committed himself to becoming single-hearted for God.*)

- What did Josiah do to show his commitment to God? (*He got rid of all the idols and made sure the people began to obey God's rules.*)

- How did this benefit Josiah and his kingdom? (*His kingdom was cleansed of the idols and evil practices and he saw the blessings of God for the duration of his life.*)

Summarize by explaining that in order to know God, we must reject the idols we depend on and worship only Him (see Exodus 20:1-4). Even though Josiah was young, he modeled this important lesson.

Option 2: Smash Up. For this option, you will need several Bibles, one copy of "Josiah: The Quick Version" (found on page 147), aluminum foil, a video recorder (a cell phone or digital camera will also work), a way to play back the recording to the group, an old blanket, safety glasses, a sledgehammer and an old tape player, CD, VCR, TV or other item that you don't mind smashing! (*Note:* These will be used to illustrate an "idol," so the greater the actual value of the item the greater the emotional impact—although you could probably pick up token idols for a few bucks at a thrift store or garage sale. You can even let the students take a swing or two if they are ready to make a similar pledge to rid their lives of idols.)

Ahead of time, record several young children's answers to the following question: "If you were made the President of the United States, what would you do?" Also ahead of time, wrap a Bible with aluminum foil and hide it somewhere in your room.

Instruct students to open their Bibles to 2 Kings 22 and explain that you will be telling the story of Josiah in a summary form, but they can still follow along in their Bibles. Read the summary of Josiah's reign from "Josiah: The Quick Version," and explain that the story of Josiah demonstrates three things we need to do to smash the idols in our lives.

First, *we need to desire God.* Explain that the first thing to note is that Josiah was thrust into a pressure situation because he was made king of a nation when he was only eight years old. His father had not left him with much of a heritage in terms of righteousness or politics, yet the Bible says that Josiah "did what was right in the eyes of the Lord" (2 Kings 22:2). Somehow, he knew that his future and the future of his kingdom depended on getting right with God. He wasn't sure exactly what that would look like, but he began by repairing the Temple of the Lord. God honored Josiah's desire to know and follow Him.

Illustrate how rare this attitude is by playing the recording of what the children you interviewed would do if they were made President of the United States. Not only will their answers be pretty cute, but the children will also most likely not mention the importance of pleasing and serving God, as Josiah was determined to do.

The second point the story of Josiah demonstrates is that *we need to discover God's Word.* Introduce this point by explaining that you've hidden a special treasure somewhere in the room, and invite students to look for it. Once the Bible (wrapped in foil) is found, continue by explaining that Josiah was determined to find out what God's Word had to say about how he and his people should be living. His reaction when he heard God's Word revealed how serious he was about knowing God and obeying His commands. He looked at his sin and at the sin of his people, immediately repented, and asked God to guide him in making changes.

The third thing the story of Josiah demonstrates is that *we need to destroy idols.* Explain that Josiah realized his life and his kingdom needed to be cleaned up before Judah could begin a fresh start with God. Throughout his kingdom,

Youth Leader Tip

Be nice to the church custodian! Keep a large tarp on hand to put down during sessions that require smashing something. This can result in a great cooperative relationship when you need extra help.

idols and evil religious practices had taken over the culture and thoughts of his people. Josiah knew that a dramatic break from idolatry had to happen, so he ordered a kingdom-wide purge of idols and false priests. Idols were smashed, burned and destroyed and evil priests were killed or chased out of Judah. As a result of Josiah's dedicated actions, the nation of Judah experienced a period of God-blessed peace and prosperity.

Illustrate the point by sharing a way in which God has helped you to break the power of an idol in your life. For example, you may have given up listening to certain kinds of music or watching certain movies or TV shows. Explain why you chose to keep your heart pure for God and how God has blessed you because of your decision (be sure to include some of the less tangible blessings: the peace that comes from knowing you did the right thing, feeling closer to God, the chance to share the change with others, and so forth).

Bring home the story of Josiah by showing students the old item you brought with you and explaining how it could be an idol in one's life. Wrap it in the blanket, put on safety glasses, and smash it with the sledgehammer. (*Note*: Please take every precaution to do this safely. Keep the item covered with the blanket, wear the safety glasses and have students stand a good distance away. When you are finished smashing the idol, dispose of the debris properly.)

DIG

Option 1: Online Idol. For this option, you will need just this awesome, wonderful, informative book! Read the following story aloud:

Alicia was a seventh-grader who received a new computer from her grandparents for her thirteenth birthday. At first she used it only a few hours a week to type out reports and papers for her history and English classes, but after about a month, she began to spend more time on the computer and use the Internet to access social networking sites.

Pretty soon, Alicia was on the computer two or three hours every day. Her parents were a little concerned with this at first, but they figured that not much harm would come from it. After all, she obviously loved it. It wasn't until the end of the semester when they realized the real harm that was being caused by Alicia spending so much time on the computer: Alicia had always gotten As and Bs, but this semester, she had gotten all Bs and Cs. The exception was an A in—you guessed it— her computer class. Now Alicia's parents don't know what to do.

Discuss the following questions:

- What advice would you give to Alicia's parents? Should they take the computer away from her? Why or why not? (*They should put limits on the amount of time Alicia is spending on the computer and place restrictions on her accessing social networking sites, at least until she can demonstrate that it no longer has a hold on her. It might be difficult to take the computer away altogether because Alicia uses it for her schoolwork.*)

- When can something good become something bad? (*When it begins to take over our lives and other good things begin to suffer.*)

- What other good things can become idols in our lives? (*Clothes, food, makeup, sports, grades, music, talents—pretty much anything.*)

- Given what we've learned about Josiah, what should we do when we recognize that something has become an idol? (*Get rid of it—at least for a while, until we feel like we can handle it without it becoming too important in our lives again.*)

Option 2: All About Idols. For this option, you will need Your Bible and some dogged determination to let students struggle with these deep questions! Discuss the following with the group:

- If God loves us no matter what, why do we need to change? (*God has proved how much He loves us by sending Jesus His Son to die for us so that we can be reconciled to God. God loves us in spite of our faults, but it's because He loves us that He wants us to get rid of the things in our lives that hurt us or keep us from being close to Him. God knows better than we do what will make us healthy, happy and fruitful. God wants to bless us, but we need to make room in our lives for His blessings.*)

- What is so bad about idols? (*God has commanded us to worship Him only [see Exodus 20:1-4] and warns us that we cannot serve two masters [see Matthew 6:24]; we must choose which we will serve. Idols cause us to value the wrong things or put too much value on neutral or even good things and steadily drift away from Him. For example, being physically fit is a good thing that God wants for us, but it's possible to attach too much of our self-esteem to our bodies and spend all our time working out or thinking about our appearance.*)

- How do we enjoy things without idolizing them? (*We need to realize that God is the giver of the gifts we enjoy, and thank Him for them [see James 1:17]. We also need to ask God and fellow Christians to let us know if we start drifting into idolatry.*)

- What should we do if we're already struggling with idols? (*God gives every Christian His Holy Spirit to overcome all temptation. Read 1 Corinthians 10:13. He has also given us a community of faith to encourage and support us.*)

- Is there anything that can never become an idol? (*Anything can become an idol—even good things such as Bible knowledge. This is because idolatry isn't just a thing; it is an attitude of our hearts. Whatever is more important than knowing and obeying God is an idol—money, entertainment, popularity, grades, our physical appearance, our possessions, and so forth. Even Bible knowledge can become idolatry when we become obsessed with merely gaining knowledge and lose sight of the God who gave it to us, not allowing His Word to help us grow in our relationship with Him.*)

APPLY

Option 1: Purging Idols. For this option, you will need nothing but this great book! (Okay, okay, we admit we're a little partial to this book!)

Begin by asking the group to think about their own homes. What is something they have that is an idol or might be on the verge of becoming an idol? If they're not sure, have them think of one thing in their room (or home) that they wouldn't want to live without for a week. This doesn't mean things they need to have to survive, such as food or water, but something like their TV, stereo, cell phone or computer. Share a personal example of something that has been an idol in your own life to help students become more introspective and vulnerable.

Ask students to get into groups of three and share about something in their own rooms that might have (or could) become idols to them—something that is more important to them than their relationship with God. Allow a few minutes for discussion, and bring the groups together and challenge students to make commitments to go without their chosen items for the next week. Acknowledge that it will be hard, but assure them that going without it for even one week will help them begin to free themselves from things that hinder their fellowship with Jesus, just as Josiah and his people became free by ridding their lives of idols.

Close in prayer, asking the Holy Spirit to give the students the strength to get rid of the idols in their lives.

Option 2: Free from Idols. For this option, you will need a ball or other sports item, a piggy bank, a school textbook, a yearbook and a makeup compact. Ahead of time, distribute the listed items around the room on various tables, chairs or pedestals.

Explain that one of the reasons people don't come to know Jesus as Savior is because they have things in their lives that are important to them and they think these things will help them meet the challenges in their lives. Point out the items you placed around the room and continue by stating that all of these things can become idols—the sports item represents special abilities or talents; the piggy bank represents financial success; the textbook represents the idol of grades or knowledge; the yearbook represents the idol of popularity and friends; the makeup represents the idol of physical appearance.

(As an option, you might want to first challenge students to stand by the item that represents something they are tempted to put their trust in more than Jesus. Give them the opportunity to silently confess this before praying for friends. Remind them that Christ will give us the strength to resist temptation when we ask Him.)

Challenge students to think of a friend who doesn't know Jesus yet and stand by the item that most accurately represents the idol that keeps that friend from coming to know Jesus. Invite students to join with anyone else standing near their chosen item in praying for their friends by name, asking God to free their friends from the idols that are keeping them from worshiping Him. If you have time, you may want to repeat this several times so that students have the chance to pray for several different friends who are trapped in idolatry.[2]

REFLECT

The following short devotions are for the students to reflect on and answer during the week. You can make a copy of these pages and distribute to your class or download and print from **www.gospellight.com/uncommon/jh_ the_old_testament.zip.**

1—IDOLS, IDOLS EVERYWHERE

How fast can you find 1 Corinthians 8:4-6?

Which of the following in the list below would be the strangest to see? (Pretty obvious, isn't it?) How about the one that would seem the most normal? (A little more difficult, huh?) How about the one that wouldn't faze you a bit?

- ❑ A woman bowing to an ATM in the middle of the mall
- ❑ Your little sister kissing a poster of her favorite actor before she leaves for school every day
- ❑ Your best friend spending all of his money to buy some CDs from his favorite band
- ❑ Your neighbor spending a whole Sunday washing, waxing and buffing his sports car

Even if you don't bow down or pray to something, it can still become an idol. How much time, thought and money do you put into little things in your life?

_____

_____

_____

Is this more time than you put toward your relationship with Jesus?

_____

_____

_____

Is there anything you need to stop worshiping today? If so, what?

_____

_____

_____

_____

2—MAKING IDOLS OUT OF PEOPLE

Be on your guard as you read 1 John 5:21.

When Will met Annie at church camp on the first night, he thought she was really funny and cute. But by Wednesday night, whoa! He was head over heels for her! He was skipping all the cabin meetings and worship times just to be with Annie and hold her hand. When the week was over and he came home, the time he used to devote to his quiet times he now spent calling Annie or writing her letters.

A lot of people think of an idol as a big, dumb statue that people bow down and give their money and things to. But really anything can be an idol, like a fancy car or even a person. An idol is anything that is more important to a person than God.

Do you have any idols in your life? If so, what are they?

_____

_____

_____

_____

Are you willing to get rid of them right now? If so, what will you do?

_____

_____

_____

_____

3—LOVE MAKES IT EASY

Hey, you! Joshua 24:19-24 is what you need to read! Hop to it!

When is it easiest to obey your parents?

- ❑ When you are really tired and just want to be left alone
- ❑ When you're worried about a big test coming up
- ❑ When you forgot to feed the dog and he is barking for some food
- ❑ When you realize how much you totally love them and want to show them that you do

It is so much easier to obey and sacrifice for someone when you feel a lot of love for them. How do you feel about God? Are you bored or tired, or are you totally in love with Him? Why?

_____

_____

_____

_____

_____

Pray that God will help you to love Him more and more as you grow with Him. The more you love Him, the more you will want to obey Him.

4—TRASH THE JUNK

Read Habakkuk 2:18-20 for a consultation of the wooden kind.

When it gets hot in Pinkerton, all the kids head out to the Pinkerton Towne Center to cool off, watch movies and drink frozen lemonades. The guys do tricks on their skateboards on the ramps and the girls giggle and look through the stores, never buying anything, just looking.

One day, Angie, a girl who loved the mall and spent a lot of time and money there, found out that her folks were getting a divorce. As soon as she heard the news, she took all the money she could find in her room ($27.48) and marched over to the mall to spend, spend, spend. What do you do when you have trouble?

- ❑ Get on the Internet?
- ❑ Go out shopping?
- ❑ Call your best friend?
- ❑ Cry by yourself in your room?
- ❑ Turn off God?

Sometimes we place way too much importance on stuff. We consider stuff more important than God, and we don't even realize we are doing it. That's called idolatry. Stop right now and ask God to help you get rid of any idols in your life that you turn to instead of turning to Him.

DANIEL: STANDING UP FOR GOD

THE BIG IDEA

Daniel lived a life of devotion, and because of this, God used him powerfully.

SESSION AIMS

In this session you will guide students to (1) learn the story of Daniel; (2) realize that his disciplined life meant clinging to some traditions and giving up others; and (3) commit themselves to doing the same.

THE BIGGEST VERSE

"But Daniel purposed in his heart that he would not defile himself" (Daniel 1:8, *NKJV*).

OTHER IMPORTANT VERSES

Psalms 119:97-104; 139; 141:5; Proverbs 12:1; Daniel 1:1-21; 2:1-49; 4:1-37; 5:1-30; 6:1-28; Matthew 14:23; Luke 18:1; John 17:16; Ephesians 4:1; Hebrews 10:24-25; 12:5-6

Note: Additional options and worksheets in 8¹/₂" x 11" format for this session are available for download at **www.gospellight.com/uncommon/jh_the_old_testament.zip**.

STARTER

Option 1: Dream a Little Dream. For this option, you will need the following dream facts. Gather together and ask students to respond to the following questions about dreaming. The answers provided will give you some scientific responses to add to their personal experiences.

- How many of you dream every night? (*Everyone dreams every night, from infants to great-grandpas and everyone in between.*)
- How many of you remember what you dreamed last night? (*Usually we don't recall a dream unless we awake immediately after we have one. Within five minutes of waking up, 90 percent of a dream memory is gone.*)
- How many of you have actually acted out a dream while you're dreaming? (*Though students may challenge you on this and say they've woken up running down the hall or jumping off a mountain, tell them their brains won't let it happen. When they sleep, their brains turn off their bodies' muscle functions—well, most of them—which means they are in a way "paralyzed" so they can't move while they're dreaming. This keeps them from actually doing what they're dreaming. An interesting side note is that sometimes a person wakes up before the body's "on switch" has fully engaged, leaving him or her unable to move for up to a minute. It's called Old Hag Syndrome because it was thought that a witch was sitting on the person, keeping them from being able to move. Scary.*)
- How many of you dream in color? (*About 10 percent of people dream in black and white even though they see colors just fine when they're awake. Even blind people dream, though often without visual images.*)
- How much of your sleep is spent dreaming? (*A typical sleep includes one to four hours of dreaming, which means that over the course of an average lifetime a person spends about six years dreaming.*)
- Do you have to dream? (*Dreams keep us mentally healthy. In one scientific study, people deprived of dreaming developed signs of psychosis within three days.*)
- How many of you can accurately interpret a dream? (*Most dreams are a function of the subconscious, so they can be very symbolic. Thus, many people have set about to offer interpretations. A lot of interpreter's think that in a dream a house represents one's own self. So, a dream about a house is a dream about oneself. Tons of people—from scientists to witch doctors—have tried to give definitive interpretations, but it's hard to say they're accurate.*)

- What does the Bible say about dreams? (*There are more than 200 references to dreams and visions in the Bible. God uses dreams to warn, to explain, to foretell, and to call. While many dreams are just a hodge-podge expression of what we've experienced in the past and what's going on right now, sometimes God gives dreams to communicate His thoughts to us directly. To that end, God usually provides not only the dream, but the interpretation too.*)

End this "dreamy" discussion by explaining that one of the most famous Bible dreamers was Daniel, which is who they will be learning about today. But be sure to add this caveat: Although God used Daniel in tremendous ways that often involved having and interpreting dreams, it was Daniel's devoted, disciplined life of faith that makes him an example for believers today.

Option 2: Stand Up If . . . For this option, you will need room to stand.

Have students sit down, and then explain that you're going to make a statement and if it applies to them, they should stand up. Try to keep the pace fairly brisk so that the students stand up, look around at the others and then sit back down without too much time between comments. You can add anything else to this list that would work well with your group.

Tell the students to stand up if they . . .

- Have a pair of white tennis shoes
- Have been surfing (add: and stood up for more than five seconds)
- Eat the inside of the Oreo first
- Share a room
- Like cottage cheese
- Play a videogame every day
- Have traveled to another state

Youth Leader Tip
One of the greatest hurdles we encounter in communicating with students is boredom. When your students see you excited and changed by God's truth they will be more responsive to what you are teaching.[1]

- Prefer baths rather than showers
- Don't use deodorant (maybe you should get someone to toss out these students)
- Own a dog (or a cat, or a bird, or a snake, or a ferret)
- Read their Bible every day
- Can recite a Bible verse (or five verses, or a whole chapter)
- Pray purposefully to God every day
- Love God more than anything or anyone else
- Would rather die than deny their faith

Have the students sit down, and then explain that a lot of times the things we stand up for are, in the grand scheme of things, pretty inconsequential (but not necessarily unimportant!). However, there are a few things that we *must* stand up for if we truly are followers of Christ—and that can be really difficult to do. Today, we will be learning about a man whose dedication and devotion to God allowed him to stand up to some fierce dangers (yes, "fierce" as in a pride of hungry lions!) and never falter in honoring the Lord. His life gives us both example and encouragement to take a stand for God.

MESSAGE

Option 1: Bloom Where You're Planted. For this option, you will need Bibles, potting soil, soil amendments, a spade, a small planter, young plants and a watering can filled with water. Ahead of time, set up the planting supplies where you can use them while you talk. (*Note*: Another option is to provide these supplies—maybe smaller plants and planters—to all your students and let them plant along with you while you talk.)

Begin by giving some background about Daniel's life. The Jews were living in Jerusalem under the reign of King Jehoiakim until Nebuchadnezzar of Babylon captured them around 586 B.C. The city itself was destroyed, and the Jews were either killed or exiled. Nebuchadnezzar had his men select the best and the brightest of the noble and royal families to be servants in his palace. Daniel was among those taken back to Babylon as a servant.

Next, state the main point: One of the great lessons we learn from Daniel's life is how to "bloom where you're planted." As you talk through Daniel's life, slowly plant the small plants in the planter: prepare the planter, mix the soil, plant the plants, water them, and so forth. It should be a long visual-aid "process" to underscore the main idea of blooming wherever we're planted.

Distribute Bibles and read aloud Daniel 1:1-7. Explain that Daniel's whole world was taken away from him: his family, his city, his independence and his routine. He was forced to become a servant in another king's court and was absorbed into a new life with new customs and different values. But rather than becoming bitter and rebellious, Daniel accepted what had happened as God's will and trusted Him to work out His purposes. *So, lesson one in blooming where you're planted is to trust that God is at work no matter what and not become bitter or scream, "It's not fair!"*

Read aloud Daniel 1:8-16. Even though Daniel was part of another culture, he didn't let go of his devotion to God. As a devoted Jew, he was used to following strict God-given rules about food—what could be eaten, how and when it could be eaten, what couldn't be eaten, and so forth. These rules were not just God being picky about food; they were a way to constantly remind His people that they were set apart from other people. Every time they put a piece of food to their lips, they remembered their unique spiritual identity, no matter where they lived on earth.[2]

So, when Daniel was offered food that went against Jewish dietary law, he didn't eat it. Without being obnoxious or surly, he simply declined and then requested to be allowed to eat as God commanded. By following God's rules, Daniel affirmed to himself and to everyone around him that he belonged to the LORD. *So, lesson two in blooming where you're planted is to hold on to your identity as a follower of Jesus.* There are some things that you can embrace, such as a new job or new clothing styles or new routines. But there are some things that you cannot give up if you want to follow Christ. The commands God gives to us in His Word involve living a different kind of life. But, like Daniel, following God's rules shouldn't make us obnoxious or rude.

Read aloud Daniel 1:17-21. Explain that because of Daniel's devotion, God blessed him and made him successful in his endeavors. His consistent dedication made him a ready instrument of blessing. God uses people who seek Him, and He gave Daniel wisdom and understanding, especially with regard to dreams and visions. This made Daniel a sought-out man; the kings he served respected him and went to him for help. Now sum up some of the major events in Daniel's life:

- Daniel was able to tell and interpret Nebuchadnezzar's first dream of the great image (see Daniel 2).
- Daniel was able to interpret Nebuchadnezzar's second dream of the tree and the beast (see Daniel 4).

- Daniel was able to read the writing on the wall during Belshazzar's feast (see Daniel 5).
- Daniel survived being thrown into the lion's den (see Daniel 6).
- Daniel received several prophetic visions about the shifting political powers of the earthly kings and the coming of God's eternal kingdom (see Daniel 7–12).

Conclude by stating that *lesson three in blooming where you're planted is to remain a consistent, dedicated, devoted follower of God and expect Him to use you.*

Hopefully, your object lesson is finished about now. Lay the spade down, brush the dirt off your hands, and encourage students that no matter what happened to him, Daniel trusted God, served well, and gave Him all the glory. They can learn from Daniel's example how to bloom right where they're planted.

Option 2: Vignettes of a Visionary. For this option, you will need Bibles.

Begin by giving some background about Daniel's life. The Jews were living in Jerusalem under the reign of King Jehoiakim until Nebuchadnezzar of Babylon captured them around 586 B.C. The city itself was destroyed and the Jews were either killed or exiled. Nebuchadnezzar had his men select the best and the brightest of the noble and royal families to be servants in his palace. Daniel was among those taken back to Babylon as a servant.

Now divide students into five groups of at least four to five students. Assign each group one of the following chapters. (*Note*: If you have fewer students, either combine or eliminate chapters.) Make sure each group has at least one Bible and explain that they will be responsible for reading the chapter together and then preparing a short skit depicting a vignette of Daniel's life and how it reflects his dedication to God. If you have enough youth leaders, assign one to work with each group to make sure students are tracking with the story and getting all the main details incorporated into their skit.

Chapter 1:   Daniel is taken to Babylon.
Chapter 2:   Daniel tells and interprets Nebuchadnezzar's first dream.
Chapter 4:   Daniel interprets Nebuchadnezzar's second dream.
Chapter 5:   Daniel explains the writing on the wall to Belshazzar.
Chapter 6:   Daniel survives a night in the lions' den.

As students present the vignettes, your job is to make their various stories into a cohesive tale of a devoted servant of God, which means you must be über familiar with all the stories. Throughout the presentations, help students see that Daniel maintained a consistent dedication to the Lord, including the disciplined habits of eating, prayer, trust and service. Daniel's consistency and godly habits allowed God to use him in many radical ways over the course of his life. Encourage students that they can experience this as well. They may not be called by God to give kings interpretations to dreams or to face a pride of hungry lions, but they will be called on to impact their world through consistent and dedicated devotion to Christ.

DIG

Option 1: Two Dreams, a Sign and a Den. For this option, you will need Bibles, copies of "Two Dreams, a Sign, and a Den" (found on the following two pages) and pens or pencils. (*Note*: A leader reference guide is included in the worksheet files that are available online for download.)

Explain that Daniel's dedication made him a vessel for God to use to show His glory to the Babylonians. Have students get into small groups and give each group at least one Bible, copies of "Two Dreams, a Sign and a Den," and pens or pencils. State that today, they will be digging into the story of Daniel to see how God used his dedicated life to impact the culture around him.

When students are finished, gather together and share what they discovered during their reading. Tie it all together by noting this similarity in all the stories: Daniel's steadfast devotion made him a witness to the one true God. Through these events, the kings and people of his new home saw that their gods were far beneath the sovereign, powerful, omniscient God that Daniel served. To underscore this, have student volunteers read aloud Daniel 2:46-47; 4:1-2,34-35 and 6:25-27, and sum up by stating that God glorified Himself through Daniel's devoted life.

Option 2: A Fasted Life. For this option, you need Bibles, copies of "A Fasted Life" (found on page 166) and pens or pencils.

Begin by explaining that Daniel is a good example of a person who lived a fasted life. He tempered *all* his activities, including his eating, in order to live a life of constant devotion to God. Sometimes, people have the wrong idea about fasting. They think it's only about not eating, as if they can bargain with God by refusing sustenance: "If I don't eat, then You have to do this . . ." But fasting is about more than having or not having food: it's about having—or not having—the right heart before God.

Two Dreams, a Sign and a Den

I. Daniel 2:1-49: Nebuchadnezzar's First Dream

What was the king's problem?

_____

_____

_____

What was Daniel's response?

_____

_____

_____

What was the result?

_____

_____

_____

II. Daniel 4:1-37: Nebuchadnezzar's Second Dream

What was the king's dream?

_____

_____

_____

Why did the king believe Daniel could interpret dreams?

_____

_____

_____

What happened to Nebuchadnezzar?

_____

_____

_____

What did Nebuchadnezzar think of Daniel's God?

_____

_____

_____

MENE
MENE
TEK

III. Daniel 5:1-30: The Writing on the Wall

What unusual event happened at the party?

_____

_____

_____

_____

Who suggested bringing in Daniel to read the message, and why did she do this?

_____

_____

_____

What did the writing mean?

_____

_____

_____

What happened in the end?

_____

_____

_____

IV. Daniel 6:1-28: Daniel in the Lions' Den

What decree was issued, and how did Daniel respond?

_____

_____

_____

How did the king feel about Daniel being thrown into the lions' den?

_____

_____

_____

How did it end?

_____

_____

_____

A Fasted Life

What does "fasting" mean?

_____

_____

_____

Can you "fast" from things other than food? If so, what?

_____

_____

Why do people fast?

_____

_____

Have you ever fasted? If so, what did you change while you were fasting?

_____

_____

What was the result of your fast?

_____

_____

Now read Daniel 9:3 and 10:3. Daniel fasted so that he could concentrate on prayer and getting wisdom from God. Why does fasting involve prayer and God's Word?

_____

_____

Read Isaiah 58:3-7. God was not pleased with His people because they thought fasting didn't need to involve their attitudes. They thought they could simply stop eating and God would be pleased. What kind of fast did God want from them?

_____

_____

Read Matthew 6:16-18. Jesus warns people not to draw attention to themselves when they are fasting. Instead, they should look happy and satisfied. Why is this important?

_____

_____

Now go back and look at your responses to the first five questions. Do you still have the same ideas about fasting? If not, what did you learn?

_____

_____

Distribute Bibles, copies of "A Fasted Life" and pens or pencils. Have students work in pairs to complete the handout. After the students have finished, gather the group together and discuss their findings. End by explaining that fasting is only a means to remind us that *all* of our appetites must be reined into total submission to God. The deprivation of fasting fosters dependence and a purposeful turning of our affections toward God. Fasting engenders surrender, and *that* is what makes it a powerful tool for spiritual growth.

Conclude by stating that Daniel surrendered his food, his time, his ambition and his daily life to God, and God used him as a witness to His sovereignty and power. Our fasted lives can do the same!

APPLY

Option 1: He Knows Me. For this option, you need copies of "He Knows Me" (found on the next page) and pens or pencils.

Begin by reminding students that sometimes when we are given a chance to stand up for God, we don't. That can make us feel disappointed in ourselves and distanced from the Lord. But God knows everything that's in us. Explain that one of the reasons Daniel was able to consistently live out his faith in God was that he was confident of God's love and faithfulness no matter what happened. Distribute "He Knows Me" and pens or pencils. Have students find a quiet place to work on the worksheet alone.

When the group members have finished, gather together and invite them to share their ideas. End by explaining that Psalm 139 teaches us that we are completely known by God. He saw us before we were born, and He knows what we will say before we say it. There isn't a single thing about us that surprises, shocks or confuses Him. Of course, when we think of a holy God knowing everything about us, we're likely to be a little scared. But the truth is that God sees everything in our hearts *and He loves us*. Daniel spent a lot time in prayer, learning to listen and obey the One who knew him best. It gave him

Youth Leader Tip

When using small groups, you may want to start by letting students share "highs" and "lows" from their week. This can get students talking, and help them relate to Daniel, who certainly had his share of "highs" and what many would call "lows."

HE KNOWS ME

Psalm 139:1-18

*You have looked deep into my heart, L*ORD*, and you know all about me.
You know when I am resting or when I am working, and from heaven you discover
my thoughts. You notice everything I do and everywhere I go. Before I even speak a word,
you know what I will say, and with your powerful arm you protect me from every side.
I can't understand all of this! Such wonderful knowledge is far above me. Where could I go
to escape from your Spirit or from your sight? If I were to climb up to the highest heavens,
you would be there. If I were to dig down to the world of the dead you would also be there.
Suppose I had wings like the dawning day and flew across the ocean. Even then your
powerful arm would guide and protect me. Or suppose I said, "I'll hide in the dark until
night comes to cover me over." But you see in the dark because daylight and dark are all
the same to you. You are the one who put me together inside my mother's body, and I praise
you because of the wonderful way you created me. Everything you do is marvelous!
Of this I have no doubt. Nothing about me is hidden from you! I was secretly
woven together deep in the earth below, but with your own eyes you saw my body
being formed. Even before I was born, you had written in your book everything I would do.
Your thoughts are far beyond my understanding, much more than I could ever imagine.
I try to count your thoughts, but they outnumber the grains of sand on the beach.
And when I awake, I will find you nearby (CEV).*

Give three examples from this passage of how well God knows you.

1. _____
2. _____
3. _____

How did the psalmist feel about the fact that God knew everything there was to know about him?

_____

_____

What were two places the psalmist said he could try to go to get away from God?

_____

_____

Underline one sentence that stands out to you from this passage. What is it about that thought that makes it stand out?

_____

_____

courage to trust that God would take care of him no matter what because He knew and loved him. God knows us as well, *and He loves us.*

Option 2: Writing on the Wall. For this option, you need Bibles, finger paints, butcher paper and masking tape. Ahead of time, tape a long segment of butcher paper up on a wall where students can easily get to it.

Explain that one of the ways God used dreams in the Bible was to foretell a coming event. (*Note:* If you didn't do so in an earlier option, read aloud Daniel 5:1-30 or sum up the details.) Explain that the writing on the wall in Daniel 5 was a merciful warning from God so that Belshazzar would repent and avoid judgment. The writing was a gift from a loving God, and it was Daniel who was given the gift of explaining it all to him.

Continue by saying that sometimes correction doesn't feel kind. We don't want to accept it when someone says, "Hey, that's wrong. Stop. Do this instead." But part of Christian life is learning to humbly receive the kindness called correction. Read aloud Psalm 141:5, Proverbs 12:1 and Hebrews 12:5-6. Discuss the connection between correction and love and how God used Daniel to speak this kindness to Belshazzar. Note to the group that, unfortunately, Belshazzar did not listen to the rebuke, and he suffered the consequence that very night.

Ask students to think about what God would write on the wall today. What loving correction would He give to them? What correction would He give to their world? Be sure to lead them in a time of helpful correction and not allow it to become a time of judgmental criticism—something that will happen if you're not prepared to direct their thinking. After this, have the group members use the finger paints to "write" those things on the butcher paper. End by praying that God would soften hearts to heed His rebuke and welcome His discipline as kindness from a loving God.

REFLECT

The following short devotions are for the students to reflect on and answer during the week. You can make a copy of these pages and distribute to your class or download and print from **www.gospellight.com/uncommon/jh_ the_old_testament.zip.**

1—GREEN-EYED MONSTERS

See what 2 Corinthians 10:12 has to say about comparing ourselves to others.

Lots of people were jealous of Daniel. After all, he was smart, handsome and well liked. Everything he did, he did well. Time and again, God used him in powerful ways. It was enough to make that green-eyed monster called jealousy a raging beast among his peers!

Jealousy is ugly and will always come back to haunt you in the end. The solution is to recognize that you are one of a kind and have a combination of gifts and talents that make you a unique and a valuable person. You don't need to spend energy wishing you were someone else. Instead, you should be spending that time developing your own gifts by seeking the One who made you.

What are three or four things that you like about yourself?

_____

_____

_____

Write out a prayer asking God to help you grow into the person He designed you to be.

_____

_____

_____

2—COMING SOON

On at least two occasions Daniel dealt with dreams about kingdoms—which country would rule and for how long. Look up Hebrews 12:28. What does this have to say about the coming of God's kingdom?

_____

_____

_____

What does Revelation 21:1-5 have to say about this?

_____

_____

_____

Daniel saw that one day God would finish everything that He had planned for this world, including setting up His everlasting kingdom. If you have placed your faith in Jesus as your Savior and you are following Him, then you are welcome into that kingdom! So how about it? Are you ready for God's eternal kingdom?

3—THE GIFT OF WONDER

People are intrigued by the supernatural. It's why stories like Daniel's are extra interesting. Seriously, who wouldn't want to be able to interpret dreams and know the future?

But have you ever stopped to consider what a gift _wonder_ is? Think about it: God could have created us with answers to everything wired in our brains from birth. He could have loaded us with all the knowledge we would ever need to know right from the start. But He didn't. Instead, we get to wonder and experience the joy that comes from finally understanding something. Instead of knowing it all, we get to seek Him for answers. In the process, we get to enjoy what He's created and how He speaks to us.

What are three things that you wonder about? (Make them good—not just "I wonder what's the next show on TV"!).

_____

_____

_____

Read 1 Corinthians 13:12. What does this say about what we will know in the future?

_____

_____

_____

Someday you will know more like the way God knows. But for now, enjoy being able to wonder. It is His gift to you!

4—PRAY, PRAY, PRAY

Read Daniel 6:10 and then fill in the missing information in the blanks:

- Daniel faced _____ when he prayed.
- Daniel was on his _____ when he prayed.
- Daniel prayed _____ times a day.
- Daniel always gave _____ when he prayed.

Daniel prayed a lot—so much so, in fact, that at one point he actually made himself kind of sick because he forgot to eat. (Have you ever prayed *that* long?) Prayer was part of his daily life; it was a habit. And God spoke powerfully to Daniel during the times he prayed.

Think about your own prayer life. When do you pray? Where do you pray? How often do you pray? What do you pray about?

_____

_____

_____

_____

How can you make prayer a more consistent part of your life? (This could be the time in which you pray, how often you pray, they way you pray, what you pray about . . .)

_____

_____

_____

_____

Some people find that writing out their prayers helps them stay on track. Some people like to kneel when they pray, because this posture tells them that they are praying. Still others find that being silent is the best way to talk with God. However you choose to pray, just remember that the *way* in which you pray isn't as important as the *fact* that you pray. So make a commitment today to pray every day. Then do it!

ESTHER: FOR SUCH A TIME AS THIS

THE BIG IDEA
Esther, a Jewish girl, remembered whose she was, and this gave her confidence to stand up for what was right.

SESSION AIMS
In this session you will guide students to (1) learn the story of Esther; (2) realize that because she clung to her identity as part of God's people she had strength to do the right thing; and (3) commit themselves to doing the same.

THE BIGGEST VERSE
"For if you remain silent at this time, relief and deliverance for the Jews will arise from another place, but you and your father's family will perish. And who knows but that you have come to royal position for such a time as this?" (Esther 4:14).

OTHER IMPORTANT VERSES
Esther 1–10; Proverbs 1:2; 2:7-8,21-22; 3:3-4,27,33-34; 5:21-22; 6:12-19; 10:7, 12,20,25,30; 11:2-3,5,8; 11:20-21; 12:4,6,10; 13:22; 14:1,19,35; 15:3,29,33; 16:3,9,13,18,33; 18:7; 19:12,20,22; 20:2,22; 21:2,7,15,30; 22:4,12; 24:16,19-20; 25:6-7,11; 26:12,24-26; 27:2; 29:6,16; 31:8-12; Ephesians 5:15; Colossians 4:5; 2 Timothy 4:2; 1 Peter 3:15

Note: Additional options and worksheets in 8^1/$_2$" x 11" format for this session are available for download at **www.gospellight.com/uncommon/jh_the_old_testament.zip**.

STARTER

Option 1: Royally Beautified. For this option, you will need two paper bags, two blindfolds, two chairs, two sets of make-up (for instance, foundations, eye shadows, lipsticks, rouges), a mirror, make-up remover, and towels. Ahead of time, divide the make-up and place it in the paper bags. Place the chairs up front facing the group.

Explain that because you will be studying the story of a drop-dead gorgeous, royal queen, you thought it appropriate that a couple of them get royally beautified. Ask for four brave volunteers—two of whom aren't afraid to get a little messy. Ask the volunteers to pair up, and then have one from each pair sit in a chair as the "royal client" and the other stand behind it as the "expert beautician."

Blindfold the expert beauticians and hand them the paper bag full of make-up. Tell them that on your signal, they are going to beautify their royal clients. The beauticians must stay blindfolded and stand behind the client the whole time; the clients in the chairs cannot move, speak or direct in any way. Give the pairs a starting signal and encourage the rest of the group to cheer on their friends. Let the pairs know that when they feel they are done, they can stop and you will remove the blindfolds so they can see their work. Use the mirror to let the volunteers see what they look like. Take a few pictures for posterity (or for Facebook), thank the students, and let them return to the group amidst wild applause and cheering.

Explain that today's lesson centers on Esther, a beautiful Jewish girl who became a brave Persian queen. When Esther first came to the palace, she spent an entire year getting beauty treatments in preparation for meeting the king—and it was time well spent because it was her beauty—of heart as well as face—that God used to soften the king's will and save the Jewish people of the day.[1]

Option 2: Golden Scepter. For this option, you will need room to run around and a golden scepter (you can substitute any staff, rod or walking stick . . . but making it gold would be nice).

Begin by telling the students that they will be looking at the story of Esther, in which a young girl bravely steps forward, hoping the king will approve her coming by holding out his golden scepter. It's a risky venture, because if he doesn't hold out the scepter, she will face death as a punishment. Ask for a volunteer to be the "king" who uses the golden scepter, and have that student go to one end of the room while everyone else moves to the opposite end as far away as possible.

Next, explain that when the king holds out his scepter toward them, they can move forward, but as soon as he pulls the scepter back, they must stop (this is very similar to the rule in Red Light-Green Light). Anyone the king sees moving will be "sentenced to death" by having to sit down until the game is over (this is when having some burly youth leaders really comes in handy!). You can play the game several times and change up things by having the students hop on one foot, crab walk, do the worm, somersault, and so on. Be sure to switch kings as well.

MESSAGE

Option 1: The Story of Esther. This option requires a bit more preparation, but it brings the story alive for the students if you can pull it off. Before the session, carefully read Esther 1–10 and be prepared to tell the whole story with style.

Begin by explaining that the book of Esther ends with a huge celebration called Purim (typically held in March). Because it is her story that inspired this celebration, one of the main customs of Purim is to read aloud the book of Esther two times, once in the morning and again in the evening. In addition to being an inspired teaching about God's providence, Esther's is an amazingly entertaining story.

Begin by stating that the hero of the tale is Esther, a beautiful young Jewess, while the villain is Haman, the king's evil advisor. Tell the students that you're going to tell them the story of Esther, but they have a job to do—something traditionally done when the story is read aloud during Purim. Every time they hear Haman's name, they should boo, stamp their feet, hiss, make noise—anything to "blot out" Haman's name. The idea is to literally drown out his name. Practice this once or twice so that students will know for sure that this is one time when it's okay to make a lot of noise during the teaching!

Now tell the story in detail. It's not long, so you can be truly Jewish about it and read portions of it straight from Scripture. If reading aloud isn't a strong

Youth Leader Tip

When you share God's word with your group, you want them to walk away saying, "Wow, I never saw that story quite like that!" If you can help students see the relevance of God's truth in their lives, they will learn that God does speak today through His Word.

point for you, then tell it as energetically and compellingly as possible (but no videos!). Here's a bare-bones outline to keep in mind, but you will need to fill in the specifics:

- The story takes place in Persia, during the fifth century B.C., where Xerxes (a.k.a. Ahasuerus) is king.
- Queen Vashti disobeys Xerxes and is dethroned. Esther, the most gorgeous girl around, becomes queen, but no one knows she is Jewish.
- Mordecai, Esther's uncle, hangs out in the palace courtyard and ends up foiling a plot to assassinate the king.
- Haman, the king's advisor, plots to kill all Jews because Mordecai won't bow down when he passes. Haman determines the day of death by casting lots, which is what *purim* means. (Haman has an ego the size of Texas.)
- At Mordecai's insistence, Esther risks death to plead for help on behalf of her people, the Jews, so they won't be destroyed. Xerxes agrees.
- The Jews are saved, Haman and his sons are hung, and Mordecai is honored.
- The day of Haman's death is turned into a day of victory and celebration. Purim is inaugurated as a yearly tradition to remember God's deliverance.

Option 2: Purim Shpiels. For this option, you will need Bibles.

Begin by explaining that the story of Esther takes place in Persia at a time when an evil man named Haman has marked the Jews of the empire for extermination for being troublemakers. Esther, the beautiful young Jewess who has become the Persian queen, risks her life to save her people—and she succeeds. The Jews celebrate a glorious victory rather than total annihilation, and they inaugurate a new holiday called Purim to commemorate their deliverance.

One of the traditions associated with Purim is the Purim Shpiel—little skits, monologues or puppet shows meant to entertain those celebrating the holiday. Shpiels can be short, funny monologues or full-out theatrical productions. Historically, some shpiels have been fairly racy and improper—that's not the intention here! You are after good, clean fun and a faithful retelling of the story.

Explain that because Esther is such a great story, they are going to stage impromptu shpiels that act out the details of the narrative. Have students get into groups of four to five. Give each group a Bible and assign them a specific section of the story of Esther to read together and then plan to act out. You can break the story down by chapter, or you can combine the chapters together if you have fewer groups. Give students 15 to 20 minutes to read and plan. The goal is to have students present the main points of the story as cohesively as possible, so it would be good to circulate around the room and offer help and clarification as needed. Here is a general breakdown of the chapters:

Chapter 1: Vashti is removed as queen.

Chapter 2: Esther becomes queen. Mordecai overhears an assassination plot against the king and tells Esther.

Chapter 3: Haman issues a decree to kill the Jews.

Chapter 4: Mordecai incites Esther to save her people.

Chapter 5: Esther goes to the king and throws a banquet.

Chapter 6: The king honors Mordecai for foiling the assassination plot against him.

Chapter 7: Esther has a second banquet, asks the king to spare her people, and points out Haman as the one who had the decree issued. Haman is put to death.

Chapter 8: The king decrees a new edict on behalf of the Jews.

Chapters 9–10: The Jews experience victory instead of extermination, and Purim is inaugurated.

DIG

Option 1: His Providence, Our Responsibility. For this option, you will need several Bibles, copies of "His Providence, Our Responsibility" (found on the next page) and pens or pencils.

Explain that the book of Esther is unique in that the name of God is never actually mentioned—not even once—yet the whole book screams His providential protection loud and clear. Throughout the story God is at work behind the scenes, setting up everything according to His perfect plan. He is sovereignly directing the events, and this teaches us to be bold in our faith and to take advantage of every opportunity He provides.

Distribute Bibles, copies of "His Providence, Our Responsibility" and pens or pencils. Explain that distinguishing between God's sovereignty and our responsibility is difficult, yet the story of Esther highlights how they work together to accomplish God's will. Today, the students are going to dig into the Word and find examples of how God's providence and our responsibility worked together in the story of Esther. Have students pair up and give them

His Providence, Our Responsibility

Skim through the book of Esther and find some ways that God worked to deliver the Jews (His providence). Then look for some of the ways people stepped up and took responsibility for their part in His plan (our responsibility). Next, write down what happened (the result). An example is provided below.

His Providence	Our Responsibility	The Result
Esther, who is a Jew, is selected as a potential replacement for Vashti.	Esther agrees to a year of beauty treatments and listens to the advice of the eunuch as to what would please the king.	Esther captures the king's heart and becomes the next queen.

time to complete the handout. Encourage each group to come up with three to four examples to share. Be sure to check in with each group once or twice and guide their efforts.

After students have found what they can, gather together and share the examples aloud. Some examples to consider are listed below, but note that there are many ways to view God's hand at work in the story.

Providence: Esther is by far the most beautiful woman around.
Responsibility: She uses her gift of beauty as a way to open doors, not as a means of personal attention.
Result: Esther gains a unique position of influence in the Persian court.

Providence: Mordecai overhears the assassination plot.
Responsibility: Mordecai tells Esther, who tells the king and essentially thwarts the plot.
Result: The king has a favorable view of the Jew Mordecai, and perhaps this extends to the Jews in general.

Providence: The king can't sleep one night so he decides to read his book of records.
Responsibility: The king realizes that Mordecai was never rewarded for revealing the assassination plot, so he makes plans to honor him.
Result: Sweet poetic justice! Haman himself ends up leading Mordecai—the man whose refusal to bow down made Haman want to exterminate all Jews—through town, shouting, "Thus shall it be done for the man whom the king wishes to honor" (Esther 6:11).

Providence: The date determined for the extermination of the Jews is the thirteenth day of the twelfth month—almost a full year away from when they cast lots.
Responsibility: Mordecai, Esther and the Jews use this time to pray and seek God's help.
Result: The Jews get the king to issue a new decree that effectively neutralizes the first and circumvents the extermination of the Jews.

Providence: Despite the custom of the day, the king welcomes Esther's coming before him uninvited and agrees to her request to come to a banquet and bring Haman.

Responsibility: She wisely arranges for an appropriate time, a private dinner party, to reveal her heritage as a Jew and to plead for the king to save her people. She also makes sure Haman, the instigator of the trouble, is present.

Result: The king is enraged that anyone would act in such a way and wants to know who it is. Esther conveniently points toward Haman.

Providence: At the end of Esther's second banquet, the king walks in on Haman just as he's throwing himself on Esther to ask for mercy.

Responsibility: The king condemns Haman to death for being a jerk . . . okay, for assaulting the queen (that's what he assumed was happening).

Result: The king orders the extermination of the evil would-be exterminator and gives all his property to Esther. She turns it over to Mordecai.

Providence: Haman's hard-hearted pride makes him act on his wife's cruel and unwise advice.

Responsibility: Haman builds a set of gallows, upon which he intends to hang Mordecai.

Result: More sweet poetic justice! Haman and his sons are hung on the very same gallows.

Option 2: Taking Advice. You will need Bibles, copies of "Taking Advice" (found on the next page) and pens or pencils. (*Note:* A leader reference guide is included in the worksheet files that are available online for download.)

Explain that the story of Esther provides wonderful examples of people who took good advice, people who took bad advice, and the outcome of both. Distribute Bibles, copies of "Taking Advice" and pens or pencils. Tell students to work in small groups to read the passages from Esther and respond to the questions. You should check in with each group as they work, making sure they are on the right track and clarifying thoughts as needed.

Youth Leader Tip
Students often feel safer sharing in small groups of at least 5 to 6. Smaller groups may make them feel like they are being put on the spot, while larger groups tend to put students in a spectator role, causing them to withdraw from participating.

Taking Advice

Read the following passages from the book of Esther and write down who gave what advice to whom and whether or not it was good (wow . . . try saying that aloud 10 times fast!).

Passage to Read	Who Gives What Advice to Whom?	Good Advice or Bad Advice? Why?
Esther 1:10-22		
Esther 2:7-11		
Esther 2:15-18		
Esther 4:11-17		
Esther 5:9-14		
Esther 6:1-12		

When students are finished, gather together and work through their answers. Use the leader reference guide to help facilitate the discussion. Note that the goal of this exercise is to help students realize that the advice they accept is often the key to their success or failure.

APPLY

Option 1: Humble Advice. For this option, you need nothing but these humble discussion questions.

Start by reminding students that it is humility that helps us keep our hearts open to God's leading and to the good advice of others. Esther's humility in accepting the wisdom of others enabled her to be used as an instrument of deliverance for her whole race. Mordecai's humility is seen in his utter dependence on God to act on behalf of the Jews. Those who prospered in the story were the ones who kept their lives in right perspective and were willing to accept God's wisdom.

Ask students to share their responses or give advice to the following questions. Assure them that discussions are not time for criticism or condemnation but for *humbly* tossing around ideas. Be sure to ask follow-up questions as needed until the students' ideas are fully explored and good advice is ringing out loud and clear. While there are no "right" answers, be sure you guide the group to consider solid, biblical responses.

- How do you know when God is asking you to do something?
- What most often stops you from obeying God?
- What's the most difficult thing you've faced involving living out your faith?
- What would you say to someone who struggles with her faith?
- What advice would you give to someone who isn't sure he believes in God?
- What's the best advice that you ever received about being a disciple of Jesus?

After you've spent time discussing these questions, pray for the students and ask God to continue to work in their lives.

Option 2: Mirrors. For this option, you will need small mirrors and an assortment of fine-tipped, colored permanent markers.

Explain that Esther had a unique gift from God that opened the door for her to save her people: her uncommon beauty. We don't often think of beauty as a gift that can serve others, because society has reframed it to be only a personal advantage that brings individual prestige. But her beauty was a gift meant for others' deliverance. God has given everyone something unique to use for His purpose and glory. That gift may be beauty as well, or it may be generosity, intelligence, musical ability, coordination, compassion, strength, wisdom— and any number of others.

Distribute a mirror to each student and place the pens out where they can be shared. Instruct students to talk about gifts they see in themselves and in others around them. This is a great time for students to affirm each other, but it's imperative that you watch closely for anyone who is not getting much feedback. Make sure *everyone* gets affirmed because everyone is gifted!

Next, have students use the markers to write across the mirror one particular gift they see in themselves. (This can be based on their own assessment or on the feedback they received from their peers.) Students can add extra designs to the mirrors if they wish. The goal is to send students home and conclude this session with a visual reminder of one gift that God has given them that they can use for His glory.

REFLECT

The following short devotions are for the students to reflect on and answer during the week. You can make a copy of these pages and distribute to your class or download and print from **www.gospellight.com/uncommon/jh_the_old_testament.zip.**

1—INWARD BEAUTY

Look up Proverbs 31:30 and 1 Peter 3:3-4 to see what the Bible has to say about beauty.

(Hey, guys: although these verses address girls specifically, the truth they teach applies to you too . . . can't help it if no men are called "beautiful" in the Bible!)

What does Proverbs 31:30 say about beauty and charm?

_____
_____
_____
_____
_____
_____

According to 1 Peter 3:3-4, where should beauty come from?

_____
_____
_____
_____
_____

Our culture places a lot of value on physical beauty, but God makes it clear that while it's nice, it isn't something to fixate on. Physical beauty *will* fade; gorgeousness *will* go away. It's things like humility, bravery and compassion that will last. Even Esther, whose beauty opened doors for her, made a lasting impact because of her humble and courageous life.

So, the next time that you look in the mirror, think about your heart as well as that adorable face of yours and ask yourself, *Which will be more beautiful in 50 years?*

2—WHOSE YOU ARE

Quick! Read 1 Peter 2:9-10 and Romans 8:1-17 to find out whose you are!

Even though Esther grew up in a foreign land, she never forgot her Jewish roots, and remembering her identity helped her save her people. So, what's your heritage? German? Spanish? Korean? Irish? A giant mixture of who-knows-what? Well, knowing your heritage is important because it helps you understand your own life and provides you with connections to many, many others. (By the way, everyone has crazy relatives, so don't worry if your lineage includes some rather . . . well . . . "interesting" people!)

Even more important than your earthly heritage is your *heavenly* one. If you are a follower of Jesus, you are part of a new family and have a wonderful heritage to enjoy! As God's child, you are now royalty and an heir to His eternal kingdom! Remembering *whose* you are is the key to living in a way that reflects your true identity as someone redeemed by the Lord.

In 1 Peter 2:9-10, how does the author describe those who have been redeemed by God?

_____

_____

_____

_____

In Romans 8:15-17, Paul states that you have been adopted by God and can call Him "Abba," which means something close to "Daddy" in English. So, write some words and tell your Dad how glad you are for your heavenly heritage.

_____

_____

_____

_____

3—TAKE A STAND

Take a stand and read Psalm 82:3-4 and Micah 6:8.

Even though it could easily have cost her life, Esther was willing to stand up for her people who were being persecuted. Look at what God says about this in the following verses and jot down a few thoughts you had while reading.

Psalm 82:3-4

_____

_____

_____

_____

Micah 6:8

_____

_____

_____

_____

There are many ways you can use your time and talents to help those who are facing difficulties. You might get involved in your church or community's homeless shelters, raise money for a Christian relief organization (such as Compassion International, Invisible Children or World Vision), or you might sit next to the kid everyone else bullies. There are always ways that you can take a stand for what is right. As a follower of Jesus, it is important to share Christ's love and make helping others a way of life. Today, pray about how God wants to use you and then write down one way you will take a stand for someone who needs help.

4—HOLY DAYS

The story of Esther ends with the beginning of a new holiday: Purim. Have you ever considered what holidays really are? Although the meaning has really gotten lost in our me-oriented society, they are literally "holy days," or days set apart for us to remember something. At Christmas, we set apart a day to remember the birth of Jesus. At Easter, we set apart a day to recall and celebrate His resurrection. Holidays aren't primarily about our enjoyment, though they often are cause for great joy. Holidays are times to turn our attention back toward events that have special significance.

What holiday is most important to you? Why?

_____

_____

_____

_____

How can you make that holiday a more meaningful "holy day"?

_____

_____

_____

_____

Celebration is important for Christians. When we gather together to remember all that the Lord has done for us, we are drawn closer to Him and to each other. And when this life is over, we will stand before the Lord and join a huge celebration of His goodness. Read Revelation 4:1-11. What are some of the events that will occur at that heavenly party?

_____

_____

_____

_____

uncommon
the mindful scholarly

A TRIBUTE TO THE LESSER-KNOWN HEROES OF THE FAITH

The men and women you studied in this unit were indeed heroes of the faith. They were individuals who were not afraid to take a stand and do amazing things for God. Yet they were not the only ones whom God used in the Old Testament to bring about His will. In fact, you may be surprised to learn the deeds of some of these other often-overlooked heroes of the faith.

Shiphrah and Puah (Exodus 1:15-21)
Shiphrah and Puah were Hebrew midwives living in Egypt before the days of Moses. Pharaoh was worried about the number of Hebrews in his land, so he instructed the midwives to kill every Hebrew boy who was born. Shiphrah and Puah, however, disobeyed this command. When asked why the babies were surviving, they gave this gutsy reply: "Hebrew women are not like Egyptian women; they are vigorous and give birth before the midwives arrive" (Exodus 1:19).

Shamgar (Judges 3:34)
Shamgar was a "judge" of Israel—a deliverer sent by God to free the Israelites from a certain enemy who was harassing them. He killed 600 Philistines with an ox-goad—a long stick with a pointy end that was usually used to guide livestock.

Jael (Judges 4:18-24)
Jael gained distinction by killing an enemy king named Sisera by driving a tent peg through his head while he slept. Ouch.

Jonathan (I Samuel 14:1-14)

We all know Jonathan as the son of King Saul and one of David's closest friends, but he was also quite a warrior in his own right. On one occasion, he and his armor-bearer snuck out of the Israelite camp and climbed up a cliff to reach an enemy Philistine outpost. When the Philistines spotted them climbing up, they said, "Come up to us and we'll teach you a lesson" (1 Samuel 14:12). However, they were the ones who got schooled that day—Jonathan and his armor bearer killed about 20 of them, causing a general panic among the Philistine army that led to their ultimate defeat.

Benaiah (I Chronicles 11:22-25)

Benaiah was a general in King David's army and also his chief bodyguard. Among his many exploits, he once went down into a pit on a snowy day and killed a lion. Most people would have been content to just let the lion sit there (job done!), but not Benaiah—crawled in after it, bad footing and all.

Omri (I Kings 16:21-28)

Omri is one of the great anti-heroes in Scripture. History records he was one of Israel's most powerful kings—so much so, in fact, that Israel was called "Omri-land" in the Assyrian records during his reign. Yet he did evil in the sight of the Lord, so the Bible gives him a grand total of eight verses covering his entire rule.

Hezekiah (2 Kings 18-20)

Hezekiah had his weaknesses as a king of Judah, but he did trust in the Lord and cleanse the land from idol worship. Later in life, Hezekiah fell ill, and the prophet Isaiah told him to get his house in order, because he was going to die. Hezekiah wept and pleaded with the Lord, so God healed him and added 15 years to his life. During his reign, Hezekiah built a tunnel to bring in water to the city of Jerusalem, which made it less vulnerable to a siege. The tunnel can still be seen today.

Ezekiel (Ezekiel 4:1-8)

Ezekiel gains distinction among the prophets because he was willing to act out God's message to the people and wasn't concerned about what many would consider to be bizarre behavior. For instance, for months at a time he lay in public on his side, bound by ropes, facing a clay model of Jerusalem.

God uses all kinds of people in all kinds of situations to do His work!

ENDNOTES

Session 1: God: The Beginning of Creation

1. The Hebrew word for God in Genesis 1:1 is *Elohim*, which is actually a plural noun. The word for "created," however, is singular. This use of the plural does not mean there are many gods. Rather, it has been called the plural of majesty or potentiality—one God, but infinite power!
2. Imagine how the words of Genesis must have sounded to the people at the time who worshiped the sun, moon, star, sky, earth, water, storm, rain, hail, light, darkness, river, tree, crop and animal gods and goddesses! Also imagine how powerful these words were to slaves who were under severe labor to a pharaoh who considered himself a god! God not only wanted to show His careful design and plan for the universe, but He also wanted the world to understand that He is the one and only Lord who alone is to be worshiped.

Session 2: Adam and Eve: The Beginning of Family

1. "Family and Social Environment," ChildStats.gov, 2009 data. http://www.childstats.gov/americaschildren/famsoc.asp.
2. Ibid.
3. In biblical times, the family unit consisted of more than just a dad, a mom, 2.5 kids and a dog. Family meant the grandparents, aunts, uncles, cousins and sometimes even servants in the household. They often lived together, or in very close proximity, and valued the benefits of the diverse and abundant family around them. Even those whose family unit had become broken through death or abandonment were pulled into the circle. God made special provision for the widows and orphans by promising to help them and place them in a family (see Psalms 10:14; 68:5,6; Proverbs 15;25; Jeremiah 49:11).
4. Jim Burns, *Uncommon Youth Ministry* (Ventura, CA: Gospel Light, 2001), p. 70.

Session 3: The Serpent: The Beginning of Sin

1. We often hear that God cursed Adam and Eve in the Garden of Eden. But read Genesis 3:14-19 a little more closely. God never cursed Adam and Eve; He cursed the serpent and the ground, but not His beloved humans. Adam and Eve—and now we—live in a cursed condition, but God did not curse the human race.
2. Leading junior-highers in a prayer of repentance should combine two elements: simplicity and sincerity. Avoid long sentences and theological wording. The idea is to provide an avenue for them to make a personal commitment to Jesus, not to feel inducted into a seminary.

Session 4: Noah: The Beginning of Worship

1. In the Old and New Testaments, the word for "worship" conveyed the idea of bowing in submission before someone—of lowering yourself before that person in respect and deference to his or her authority. This outward posture of lowering yourself reflects the inward attitude of respect and honor for the one being worshiped and explains why the worship of God is not just singing a song or following a liturgy. The worship of God is a conscientious act of submission to the King of all kings and an outflowing of our heart's cry of thankfulness to Him. We worship God by deferring to His will and obeying His Word over our own.
2. Jim Burns, *Uncommon Stories and Illustrations* (Ventura, CA: Gospel Light, 2008), p. 154.
3. A worship resource that you might find helpful is *Uncommon Worship Experiences* (Ventura, CA: Gospel Light, 2010).

Session 5: Abraham: The Beginning of Faith

1. Haran was located about 400 miles northeast of Canaan. Situated on the Balikh River, it was an important junction on the caravan route between Nineveh, Carchemish, Mesopotamia, the Hittite Empire and Egypt.

Session 6: Joseph: The Beginning of Deliverance
1. Joseph was the eleventh son of Jacob and the first-born son of Rachel. Like his father, Jacob, and grandfather, Isaac, Joseph was born to a woman who had previously been barren. The highlighting of this fact in Scripture helps to impress upon us the divine activity in connection with his birth.
2. Augustine once said, "The Old Testament revealed in the New, the New veiled in the Old." For the Christian, Christ is the theme of *both* Testaments. Many Old Testament events, such as this story of Joseph, pre-figure an aspect of Christ and His revelation in the New Testament.

Session 7: Moses: Delivering God's People
1. An example that you could show is "Luckiest Man Alive," found at http://www.youtube.com/watch?v=AZCiXzm97SM&feature=related.
2. When God called out to Moses from the burning bush, He told Moses to not come any closer but to take off his sandals as a sign of worship (see Exodus 3:5). This might have originated as a sign of acceptence of a servant's position, as slaves typically went barefoot (see Luke 15:22). Notice also that God says that Moses is on "holy" ground, which is the first occurence of the word in the Bible. The ground was made holy by the presence of God and the revelation about Himself that He would make at that location.

Session 8: Samuel: Obeying God's Voice
1. In an ironic twist, when Samuel grew older, his sons followed the path of Eli's sons and were involved in dishonest acts and bribery (see 1 Samuel 8:1-3). Because of Samuel's age and his sons' dishonesty, the elders of Israel asked him to appoint a king, which ultimately led to Saul being anointed as king. This initiated a series of kings, some of whom were godly and some who were not, and resulted in the eventual division of Israel into two kingdoms.

Session 9: David: Seeking After God's Heart
1. The Philistines are believed to have been culturally related to the Mycenean or proto-Greek world and originated from Crete. They conquered the local Caananite western-Semitic speaking population of the coast, and together the conquered people and the invaders created a blended culture. The Philistines made frequent incursions against the Israelites, and there was almost perpetual war between the two peoples.
2. In 1 Samuel 24:1:5, Saul is relieving himself in a cave in which David and his men happen to be hiding. David creeps up to him and cuts off a piece of his robe. In 1 Samuel 26:1-12, David sneaks into Saul's camp at night, finds Saul sleeping there, and takes his spear and water jug.

Session 10: Josiah: Getting Rid of Idols
1. Adapted from the *San Jose Mercury News*, July 4, 1988.
2. For additional information on dealing with idolatry, see Neil T. Anderson and Dave Park, *Stomping Out the Darkness* (Ventura, CA: Gospel Light, 2008) and *Busting Free* (Ventura, CA: Gospel Light, 2010).

Session 11: Daniel: Standing Up for God
1. Jim Burns, *Uncommon Youth Ministry* (Ventura, CA: Gospel Light, 2001), p. 205.
2. In the ancient world, to share a meal was to commit oneself to friendship. By rejecting this food, Daniel might have been rejecting this symbol of dependence on King Nebuchadnezzar in order to be free to fulfill his primary obligations to God.

Session 12: Esther: For Such a Time as This
1. The book of Esther does not mention the name of God—a fact that has caused some trouble among theologians (including Martin Luther, who believed it shouldn't be included in the books of the Old Testament). However, the entire book clearly shows that God's guiding hand was behind the scenes to save the Jewish nation. It also teaches us to expect that God is at work in our present circumstances, just as He was with His people.